ArcPy and ArcGIS – Geospatial Analysis with Python

Use the ArcPy module to automate the analysis and mapping of geospatial data in ArcGIS

Silas Toms

PACKT PUBLISHING

BIRMINGHAM - MUMBAI

ArcPy and ArcGIS – Geospatial Analysis with Python

First published: February 2015

Production reference: 1210215

Published by Packt Publishing Ltd.
Livery Place
35 Livery Street
Birmingham B3 2PB, UK.

ISBN 978-1-78398-866-2

www.packtpub.com

Credits

Author
Silas Toms

Reviewers
Alessio Di Lorenzo
Dara O'Beirne
Mark Pazolli
Marjorie Roswell

Commissioning Editor
Ashwin Nair

Acquisition Editor
Harsha Bharwani

Content Development Editor
Akashdeep Kundu

Technical Editor
Deepti Tuscano

Copy Editors
Aarti Saldanha
Adithi Shetty

Project Coordinator
Milton Dsouza

Proofreaders
Simran Bhogal
Joanna McMahon
Bernadette Watkins

Indexer
Priya Sane

Production Coordinator
Alwin Roy

Cover Work
Alwin Roy

About the Author

Silas Toms is a geospatial programmer and analyst with a love of geography, history, food, and sports. He resides in the San Francisco Bay Area and can't decide which side of the Bay is more beautiful. He received a bachelor's degree in Geography from Humboldt State University and is currently pursuing a master's degree in GIS at San Francisco State University. With a background in GIS analysis for city governments and environmental consulting, Silas loves the combination of GIS and Python for analysis automation and data manipulation.

Working for Arini Geographics, Silas is helping governments understand how GIS can organize and simplify the management of infrastructure and the environment. This dual role as a programmer and analyst allows him to use Python and GIS to quickly produce geospatial data and tools. Combined with web mapping, these tools are transforming how governments work to serve the public. He also teaches workshops on ArcPy and web mapping at the City College of San Francisco, while hoping to one day finish his master's thesis.

Silas has worked as a reviewer on the book *Python Geospatial Analysis, Packt Publishing* and is working on the book *Python Geospatial Development, Packt Publishing* to be published in 2015.

I would like to thank my girlfriend, Christine, for her encouragement and patience. I would like to thank my boss, Gabriel Paun, for his inspiration and for pushing me to become a true GIS professional. I would like to thank the faculty at HSU and SFSU for their help along the way, and I would like to thank my family for their belief in me and for never asking me if I was going to become a teacher with my geography degree (even though I have and I love it!).

About the Reviewers

Alessio Di Lorenzo is a marine biologist and has an MSc in Geographical Information Systems (GIS) and Remote Sensing. Since 2006, he has been dealing with the analysis and development of GIS applications dedicated to the study and spread of environmental and epidemiological data. He is experienced in the use of the main proprietary and open source GIS software and programming languages.

Dara O'Beirne is a certified GIS Professional (GISP) with over eight years of GIS and Python experience. Dara earned both his Bachelors and Masters of Arts degrees in geography from San Francisco State University. Dara is currently a GIS Analyst working at Arini Geographics in Santa Clara, CA. Before joining Arini Geographics, Dara was a GIS Analyst and technical lead at Towill Inc., a GIS and Land Surveying company in Northern California. At Towill, Dara played a central role in developing and implementing procedures related to the collection and analysis of LiDAR data for environmental and engineering applications. Prior to Towill, Dara gained his professional GIS experience working for the Golden Gate National Recreation Area managed by the National Park Service, one of the largest urban park systems in the world, which includes National treasures, such as Alcatraz, Muir Woods, and the Marin Headlands. His Master's Thesis examined the errors associated with measuring tree heights in an urban environment with both traditional field methods and airborne LiDAR data.

I would like to thank my wife, Kate, and daughter, Anya O'Beirne, for their patience and assistance during the review of this book.

Marjorie Roswell is a web developer and map maker from Baltimore, MD. She purchased her first GIS in 1991, and built an application to assist citizen callers to the Baltimore Office of Recycling. Recent projects include interactive maps of legislative scores, political endorsements, committees, election data, and advocacy interests.

Her site `http://committeemaps.org/` details Congressional committee membership, while the site `http://farmbillprimer.org/` is devoted to mapping and charting federal food and farm policy.

Marjorie is the author of *Drupal 5 Views Recipes, Packt Publishing*. She was the technical reviewer of *jQuery UI 1.10, The User Interface Library for jQuery, Packt Publishing*.

Mark Pazolli is an engineer and data scientist who uses ArcGIS and Python to help his employers decipher the mountains of data they keep on the assets of the Western Australian electrical network. He has qualifications in Electrical Engineering, Computer Science, and Applied Mathematics. He appreciates excellent design and enjoys building interesting things.

www.PacktPub.com

Support files, eBooks, discount offers, and more

For support files and downloads related to your book, please visit www.PacktPub.com.

Did you know that Packt offers eBook versions of every book published, with PDF and ePub files available? You can upgrade to the eBook version at www.PacktPub.com and as a print book customer, you are entitled to a discount on the eBook copy. Get in touch with us at service@packtpub.com for more details.

At www.PacktPub.com, you can also read a collection of free technical articles, sign up for a range of free newsletters and receive exclusive discounts and offers on Packt books and eBooks.

https://www2.packtpub.com/books/subscription/packtlib

Do you need instant solutions to your IT questions? PacktLib is Packt's online digital book library. Here, you can search, access, and read Packt's entire library of books.

Why subscribe?

- Fully searchable across every book published by Packt
- Copy and paste, print, and bookmark content
- On demand and accessible via a web browser

Free access for Packt account holders

If you have an account with Packt at www.PacktPub.com, you can use this to access PacktLib today and view 9 entirely free books. Simply use your login credentials for immediate access.

Table of Contents

Preface

ArcGIS, the GIS software from industry leader ESRI, allows for the analysis and presentation of geospatial data.

The integration of Python into ArcGIS has made the ArcPy module an important tool for GIS students and professionals. The ArcPy module provides a powerful way to improve productivity when performing geospatial analysis. From basic Python scripting through advanced ArcPy methods and properties, ArcPy and other Python modules will improve the speed and repeatability of any GIS work flow.

This book will guide you from basic Python scripting to advanced scripting tools. It focuses on geospatial analysis scripting and touches on automating cartographic output. By the end of this book, you will be able to create reusable modules, add repeatable analyses as script tools in ArcToolbox, and export maps automatically. By reducing the time-consuming nature of GIS from days to hours, one GIS professional can become as powerful as a whole team.

What this book covers

Chapter 1, Introduction to Python for ArcGIS, offers a quick introduction to the basics of Python, including other uses for the programming language. It covers Python data types and important modules used throughout the book.

Chapter 2, Configuring the Python Environment, is an introduction to how Python works: its folder structure, executables, and modules. It also explains importing modules into scripts, the built-in modules, and covers Integrated Development Environments (IDEs), which are powerful programming aids.

Chapter 3, Creating the First Python Script, demonstrates how to use ArcGIS ModelBuilder to model the first analysis and then export it as a Python script. String manipulations and how to use file paths in Python are also introduced.

Chapter 4, Complex ArcPy Scripts and Generalizing Functions, examines how to perform analyses and produce outputs that are not possible using ModelBuilder. By using functions, or reusable code blocks, repeating code is avoided.

Chapter 5, ArcPy Cursors – Search, Insert, and Update, covers ArcPy data access cursors and how they are used to search, update, or insert records in feature classes and tables. It explains the quirks of iterating using cursors, and how to only select or update the records of interest.

Chapter 6, Working with ArcPy Geometry Objects, explores ArcPy Geometry objects and how they are combined with cursors to perform spatial analysis. It demonstrates how to buffer, clip, reproject, and more using the data cursors and the Arcpy geometry types without using ArcToolbox.

Chapter 7, Creating a Script Tool, explains how to make scripts into tools that appear in ArcToolbox and are dynamic in nature. It explains how the tools and scripts communicate and how to set up the ArcTool dialog to correctly pass parameters to the script.

Chapter 8, Introduction to ArcPy.Mapping, explores the powerful Arcpy.Mapping module and how to fix broken layer links, turn layers on and off, and dynamically adjust titles and text. It shows how to create dynamic map output based on a geospatial analysis.

Chapter 9, More ArcPy.Mapping Techniques, introduces Layer objects, and their methods and properties. It demonstrates how to control map scales and extents for data frames, and covers automated map export.

Chapter 10, Advanced Geometry Object Methods, expands on the ArcPy Geometry object methods and properties. It also explains how to create a module to save code for reuse in subsequent scripts, and demonstrates how to create Excel spreadsheets containing results from a geospatial analysis.

Chapter 11, Network Analyst and Spatial Analyst with ArcPy, introduces the basics of using ArcPy for advanced geospatial analysis using the ArcGIS for Desktop Network Analyst and Spatial Analyst Extensions.

Chapter 12, The End of the Beginning, covers other important topics that need to be understood to have a full grasp of ArcPy. These topics include the Environment Settings, XY values and Z and M resolutions, Spatial Reference Systems (Projections), the Describe functions, and more.

What you need for this book

You will need the proprietary or free version of ArcGIS 10.1/10.2/10.3. To support your environment, you will need 2GB RAM, 32-bit or 64 bit machine hardware configuration, and Windows 7/8. Python 2.7 is required to do the programming and is installed along with ArcGIS.

Who this book is for

This book is intended for GIS students and professionals who need an understanding of how to use ArcPy to reduce repetitive tasks and perform analysis faster. It is also a valuable book for Python programmers who would like to understand how to automate geospatial analysis using the industry standard ArcGIS software and its ArcPy module.

Conventions

In this book, you will find a number of styles of text that distinguish between different kinds of information. Here are some examples of these styles, and an explanation of their meaning.

Code words in text, database table names, folder names, filenames, file extensions, pathnames, dummy URLs, user input, and Twitter handles are shown as follows: "The two data pieces, the BusStopID and the `averatePop` variable are then added to a list."

A block of code is set as follows:

```
with arcpy.da.SearchCursor(Intersect71Census, ["STOPID","POP10"]) as
cursor:
    for row in cursor:
        busStopID = row[0]
        pop10 = row[1]
        if busStopID not in dataDictionary.keys():
            dataDictionary[busStopID] = [pop10]
        else:
            dataDictionary[busStopID].append(pop10)
```

Any command-line input or output is written as follows:

```
>>> aString = "This is a string"
>>> bString = " and this is another string"
>>> aString + bString
```

New terms and **important words** are shown in bold. Words that you see on the screen, in menus or dialog boxes for example, appear in the text like this: "Select it by clicking on it, and then clicking on the **Edit** button."

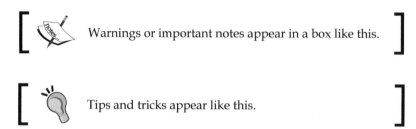

Warnings or important notes appear in a box like this.

Tips and tricks appear like this.

Reader feedback

Feedback from our readers is always welcome. Let us know what you think about this book—what you liked or may have disliked. Reader feedback is important for us to develop titles that you really get the most out of.

To send us general feedback, simply send an e-mail to feedback@packtpub.com, and mention the book title via the subject of your message.

If there is a topic that you have expertise in and you are interested in either writing or contributing to a book, see our author guide on www.packtpub.com/authors.

Customer support

Now that you are the proud owner of a Packt book, we have a number of things to help you to get the most from your purchase.

Downloading the example code

You can download the example code files for all Packt books you have purchased from your account at http://www.packtpub.com. If you purchased this book elsewhere, you can visit http://www.packtpub.com/support and register to have the files e-mailed directly to you.

Downloading the color images of this book

We also provide you with a PDF file that has color images of the screenshots/ diagrams used in this book. The color images will help you better understand the changes in the output. You can download this file from `http://www.packtpub.com/ sites/default/files/downloads/8662OS_ColorImages.pdf`.

Errata

Although we have taken every care to ensure the accuracy of our content, mistakes do happen. If you find a mistake in one of our books—maybe a mistake in the text or the code—we would be grateful if you could report this to us. By doing so, you can save other readers from frustration and help us improve subsequent versions of this book. If you find any errata, please report them by visiting `http://www.packtpub. com/submit-errata`, selecting your book, clicking on the **Errata Submission Form** link, and entering the details of your errata. Once your errata are verified, your submission will be accepted and the errata will be uploaded to our website or added to any list of existing errata under the Errata section of that title.

To view the previously submitted errata, go to `https://www.packtpub.com/books/ content/support` and enter the name of the book in the search field. The required information will appear under the **Errata** section.

Piracy

Piracy of copyright material on the Internet is an ongoing problem across all media. At Packt, we take the protection of our copyright and licenses very seriously. If you come across any illegal copies of our works, in any form, on the Internet, please provide us with the location address or website name immediately so that we can pursue a remedy.

Please contact us at `copyright@packtpub.com` with a link to the suspected pirated material.

We appreciate your help in protecting our authors, and our ability to bring you valuable content.

Questions

You can contact us at `questions@packtpub.com` if you are having a problem with any aspect of the book, and we will do our best to address it.

1
Introduction to Python for ArcGIS

In this chapter, we will discuss the development of Python as a programming language, from its beginning in the late 1980s to its current state. We will discuss the philosophy of design that spurred its development, and touch on important modules that will be used throughout the book, especially focusing on the modules built into the Python standard library. This overview of the language and its features will help explain what makes Python a great language for ArcGIS automation.

This chapter will cover:

- A quick overview of Python: What it is and does, who created it, and where it is now
- The ArcPy module and other important modules
- Python as a general purpose programming language

Overview of Python

Python, created by *Guido van Rossum* in 1989, was named after his favorite comedy troupe, Monty Python. His work group at the time had a tradition of naming programs after TV shows, and he wanted something irreverent and different from its predecessors - ABC, Pascal, Ada, Eiffel, FORTRAN, and others. So he settled on Python, feeling it was a bit edgy and catchy as well. It's certainly more fun to say than C, the language on which Python is based.

Today, Python is a major programming language. It is used in web development, database administration, and even to program robots. Most importantly to GIS Analysts, Python can be used to control ArcGIS tools and Map Documents to produce geospatial data and maps in an organized and speedy manner using the excellent **ArcPy** module.

ArcPy is installed with ArcGIS for desktop and ArcGIS for server. ArcPy has been the official ArcGIS scripting language since ArcGIS 10.0 and has steadily improved in functionality and implementation. This book will target ArcGIS for Desktop 10.1 and later, and will demonstrate how to make use of Python and its powerful programming libraries (or modules) when crafting complex geospatial analyses.

Python as a programming language

Over the past 40 years, programming languages have developed from assembly and machine code towards high-level abstracted languages that are much closer to English. The Python programming language was designed to overcome many issues that programmers were complaining about in the 1980s: slow development time, overly complicated syntax, and horrible readability. *Van Rossum* wanted to develop a language that could enable rapid code development and testing, have simple or at least readable) syntax, and produce results with fewer lines of code, in less time. The first version of Python (0.9.0) was released in 1991 and was freely obtainable from the start; Python was open source before the term open source was invented.

Interpreted language

Python is an interpreted language. It is written in C, a compiled language, and the code is interpreted from Python into C before it is executed. Practically, this means that the code is executed as soon as it is converted and compiled. While code interpretation can have speed implications for the execution of Python-based programs, the faster development time allowed by Python makes this drawback easy to ignore. Testing of code snippets is much faster in an interpretive environment, and it is perfect to create scripts to automate basic, repeatable computing tasks. Python scripts have the .py extentions. Once the code has been interpreted, a second Python script (with the .pyc extentions) is generated to save the compiled code. The .pyc script will be automatically recompiled when changes are made in the original .py script.

Standard (built-in) library

Python, when installed, has a basic set of functionality that is referred to as the standard library. These tools allow Python to perform string manipulations, math computations, and HTTP calls and URL parsing, along with many other functions. Some of the tool libraries, known to Python programmers as modules, are built-in and available as soon as Python is started, while others must be explicitly called using the `import` keyword to make their functions and classes available. Other modules have been developed by third parties and can be downloaded and installed onto the Python installation as needed.

Many new programmers wonder if Python is a real programming language, which is a loaded question. The answer is yes; Python can be used to create complete programs, build websites, run computer networks, and much more. The built-in modules and add-on modules make Python very powerful, and it can be (and has been) used for nearly any part of a computer — operating systems, databases, web servers, desktop applications, and so on. It is not always the best choice for the development of these tools, but that has not stopped programmers from trying and even succeeding.

The glue language

Python is at its best when it is used as a glue language. This term describes the use of Python to control other programs, sending inputs to them and collecting outputs, which are then sent to another program or written to disk. An ArcGIS example would be to use Python to download zipped shapefiles from a website, unzipping the files, processing the files using ArcToolbox, and compiling the results into an Excel spreadsheet. All of this is accomplished using freely available modules that are either included in Python's standard library, or added when ArcGIS is installed.

Wrapper modules

The ArcPy module is a wrapper module. Wrapper modules are common in Python, and are so named because they wrap Python onto the tools we will need. They allow us to use Python to interface with other programs written in C or other programming languages, using the **Application Programming Interface (API)** of those programs. For example, wrappers make it possible to extract data from an Excel spreadsheet and transform or load the data into another program, such as ArcGIS. Not all modules are wrappers; some modules are written in pure Python and perform their analysis and computations using the Python syntax. Either way, the end result is that a computer and its programs are available to be manipulated and controlled using Python.

The *Zen of Python* was created to be straightforward, readable, and simplified, compared to other languages that existed previously. This governing philosophy was organized into a poem by *Tim Peters*, an early Python developer called the *Zen of Python*; it is an Easter egg (a hidden feature) included in every Python installation and is shown when `import this` is typed in the Python interpreter:

```
The Zen of Python, by Tim Peters:
Beautiful is better than ugly.
Explicit is better than implicit.
Simple is better than complex.
Complex is better than complicated.
Flat is better than nested.
Sparse is better than dense.
Readability counts.
Special cases aren't special enough to break the rules.
Although practicality beats purity.
Errors should never pass silently.
Unless explicitly silenced.
In the face of ambiguity, refuse the temptation to guess.
There should be one-- and preferably only one --obvious way to do
Although that way may not be obvious at first unless you're Dutch.
Now is better than never.
Although never is often better than *right* now.
If the implementation is hard to explain, it's a bad idea.
If the implementation is easy to explain, it may be a good idea.
Namespaces are one honking great idea -- let's do more of those!
```

Go to `https://www.python.org/doc/humor/` for more information.

The basics of Python

Python has a number of language requirements and conventions that allow for the control of modules and structuring of code. The following are a number of important basic concepts, which will be used throughout this book and when crafting scripts for use with geospatial analyses.

Import statements

Import statements are used to augment the power of Python by calling other modules for use in the script. These modules can be part of the standard Python library of modules, such as the math module (used to do higher mathematical calculations) or, importantly, ArcPy, which will allow us to interact with ArcGIS.

 `Import` statements can be located anywhere before the module is used, but by convention, they are located at the top of a script.

There are three ways to create an `import` statement. The first, and most standard, is to import the whole module as follows:

```
import arcpy
```

- Using this method, we can even import more than one module on the same line. The following imports three modules: `arcpy`, `os` (the operating system module), and `sys` (the Python system module):

```
import arcpy, os, sys
```

- The next method of importing a script is to import a specific portion of a module, instead of importing the entire module, using the `from <module> import <submodule>` syntax:

```
from arcpy import mapping
```

- This method is used when only a portion of the code from ArcPy will be needed; it has the practical effect of limiting the amount of memory used by the module when it is called. We can also import multiple portions of the module in the same fashion:

```
from arcpy import mapping, da
```

- The third way to import a module is the `from <module> import <submodule>` syntax, but by using an asterisk to import all parts of the module:

```
from arcpy import *
```

This last method is still used but it is discouraged as it can have unforeseen consequences. For instance, the names of the variables in the module might conflict with another variable in another module if they are not explicitly imported. For this reason, it is best to avoid this third method. However, lots of existing scripts include import statements of this type so be aware of these consequences.

Variables

Variables are a part of all programming languages. They are used to reference data and store it in memory for use later in a script. There are a lot of arguments over the best method to name variables. No standard has been developed for Python scripting for ArcGIS. The following are some best practices to use when naming variables.

- **Make them descriptive**: Don't just name a variable *x*; that variable will be useless later when the script is reviewed and there is no way to know what it is used for, or why. They should be longer rather than shorter, and should hint at the data they reference or even the data type of the object they reference:

    ```
    shapefilePath = 'C:/Data/shapefile.shp'
    ```

- **Use camel case to make the variable readable**: Camel case is a term used for variables that start with a lower case letter but have upper case letters in the middle, resembling a camel's hump:

    ```
    camelCase = 'this is a string'
    ```

- **Include the data type in the variable name**: If the variable contains a string, call it variableString. This is not required, and will not be used dogmatically in this book, but it can help organize the script and is helpful for others who will read these scripts. Python is *dynamically* typed instead of *statically*. A programming language distinction means that a variable does not have to be declared before it can be used, unlike Visual Basic or other statically typed languages. This improves the speed of writing a script, but it can be problematic in long scripts as the data type of a variable will not be obvious.

 The ArcGIS does not use camel case when it exports Python scripts, and many examples will not include it; nevertheless, it is recommended when writing new scripts. Also, variables cannot start with a number.

For loops

Built into programming languages is the ability to iterate, or perform a repeating process, over a dataset to transform or extract data that meets specific criteria. Python's main iteration tool is known as a `for` loop. The term `for` loop means that an operation will loop, or iterate, over the items in a dataset to perform the operation on each item. The dataset must be iterable to be used in a `for` loop, a distinction discussed further ahead.

We will be using for loops throughout this book. Here is a simple example that uses the Python Interpreter to take string values and print them in an uppercase format, using a for loop:

```
>>> newlist = [ 'a' , 'b' , 'c' , 'd' ]
>>> for item in newlist:
  print item.upper()
```

The output is shown as follows:

```
A
B
C
D
```

The variable item is a generic variable assigned to each object as it is entered into the for loop, and not a term required by Python. It could have been x or value instead. Within the loop, the first object (a) is assigned to the generic variable item and has the upper string function applied to it to produce the output A. Once this action has been performed, the next object (b) is assigned to the generic variable to produce an output. This loop is repeated for all members of the dataset newlist; once completed, the variable item will still carry the value of the last member of the dataset (d in this case).

Downloading the example code

You can download the example code files for all Packt books you have purchased from your account at http://www.packtpub.com. If you purchased this book elsewhere, you can visit http://www.packtpub. com/support and register to have the files e-mailed directly to you.

If/Elif/Else statements

Conditional statements, called if/else statements in Python, are also standard in programming languages. They are used when evaluating data; when certain conditions are met, one action will be taken (the initial if statement; if another condition is met, another action is taken; this is an `elif` statement), and if the data does not meet the condition, a final action is assigned to deal with those cases (the else statement). These are similar to a where conditional in a SQL statement used with the Select tool in ArcToolbox. Here is an example of how to use an if/else statement to evaluate data in a list (a data type discussed further ahead) and find the remainder when divided using the modulus operator (%) and Python's is equal to operator (==):

```
>>> data = [1,2,4,5,6,7,10]
>>> for val in data:
    if val % 2 == 0:
    print val,"no remainder"
    elif val % 3 == 2:
    print val, "remainder of two"
    else:
        print "final case"
```

The output is shown as follows:

```
final case
2 no remainder
4 no remainder
5 remainder of two
6 no remainder
final case
10 no remainder
```

While statements

Another important evaluation tool is the `while` statement. It is used to perform an action while a condition is true; when the condition is false, the evaluation will stop. Note that the condition must become false, or the action will be always performed, creating an infinite loop that will not stop until the Python interpreter is shut off externally. Here is an example of using a while loop to perform an action until a true condition becomes false:

```
>>> x = 0
>>> while x < 5:
    print x
    x+=1
```

The output is shown as follows:

```
0
1
2
3
4
```

Comments

Comments in Python are used to add notes within a script. They are marked by a pound sign, and are ignored by the Python interpreter when the script is run. Comments are useful to explain what a code block does when it is executed, or to add helpful notes that script authors would like future script users to read:

```
# This is a comment
```

While it is a programming truism that good code is well-commented code, many programmers skip this valuable step. Also, too many comments can reduce their usefulness and the script's readability. If variables are descriptive enough, and code is well-organized, comments are less necessary; writing the code as verbose and as well-organized as possible will require less time to be spent on comments.

Data types

GIS uses points, lines, polygons, coverages, and rasters to store data. Each of these GIS data types can be used in different ways when performing an analysis and have different attributes and traits. Python, similar to GIS, has data types that organize data. The main data types in Python are strings, integers, floats, lists, tuples, and dictionaries. They each have their own attributes and traits (or properties), and are used for specific parts of code automation. There are also built-in functions that allow for data types to be converted (or casted) from one type to another; for instance, the integer 1 can be converted to the string 1 using the str() function:

```
>>> variable = 1
>>> newvar = str(variable)
>>> newvar
```

The output is shown as follows:

1

Strings

Strings are used to contain any kind of character. They begin and end with quotation marks, with either single or double quotes used, though the string must begin and end with the same type of quotation marks. Within a string, quoted text can appear; it must use the opposite quotation marks to avoid conflicting with the string.Check the following example:

```
>>> quote = 'This string contains a quote: "Here is the quote" '
```

A third type of string is also employed, a multiple line string that starts and ends with three single quote marks:

```
>>> multiString = '''This string has

multiple lines and can go for

as long as I want it too'''
```

Integers

Integers are whole numbers that do not have any decimal places. There is a special consequence to the use of integers in mathematical operations; if integers are used for division, an integer result will be returned. Check out this code snippet below to see an example of this:

```
>>> 5 / 2
```

The output is shown as follows:

2

Instead of an accurate result of 2.5, Python will return the floor value, or the lowest whole integer for any integer division calculation. This can obviously be problematic and can cause small bugs in scripts that can have major consequences.

 Please be aware of this issue when writing scripts and use floats to avoid it as described in the following section.

Floats

Floating point values, or floats, are used by Python to represent decimal values. The use of floats when performing division is recommended:

```
>>> 5.0 / 2
```

The output is shown as follows:

```
2.5
```

Because computers store values in a base 2 binary system, there can be issues representing a floating value that would normally be represented in a base 10 system. Read `docs.python.org/2/tutorial/floatingpoint.html` for a further discussion of the ramifications of this limitation.

Lists

Lists are ordered sets of data that are contained in square brackets ([]). Lists can contain any other type of data, including other lists. Data types can be mixed within a single list. Lists also have a set of methods that allow them to be extended, reversed, sorted, summed, or extract the maximum or minimum value, along with many other methods. Data pieces within a list are separated by commas.

List members are referenced by their index, or position in the list, and the index always starts at zero. Look at the following example to understand this better:

```
>>> alist = ['a','b','c','d']
>>> alist[0]
```

The output is shown as follows:

```
'a'
```

This example shows us how to extract the first value (at the index 0) from the list called `alist`. Once a list has been populated, the data within it is referenced by its index, which is passed to the list in square brackets. To get the second value in a list (the value at index 1), the same method is used:

```
>>> alist[1]
```

The output is shown as follows:

```
'b'
```

To merge two lists, the `extend` method is used:

```
>>> blist = [2,5,6]
>>> alist.extend(blist)
>>> alist
```

The output is shown as follows:

```
['a', 'b', 'c', 'd', 2, 5, 6]
```

Tuples

Tuples are related to lists and are denoted by parentheses (()). Unlike lists, tuples are immutable—they cannot be adjusted or extended once they have been created. Data within a tuple is referenced in the same way as a list, using index references starting at zero:

```
>>> atuple = ('e','d','k')
>>> atuple[0]
```

The output is shown as follows:

```
'e'
```

Dictionaries

Dictionaries are denoted by curly brackets ({}) and are used to create `key:value` pairs. This allows us to map values from a key to a value, so that the value can replace the key and data from the value can be used in processing. Here is a simple example:

```
>>> adic = {'key':'value'}
>>> adic['key']
```

The output is shown as follows:

```
'value'
```

Note that instead of referring to an index position, such as lists or tuples, the values are referenced using a key. Also, keys can be any other type of data except lists (because lists are mutable).

This can be very valuable when reading a shapefile or feature class. Using an ObjectID as a key, the value would be a list of row attributes associated with ObjectID. Look at the following example to better understand this behavior:

```
>>> objectIDdic = { 1 : [ '100' , 'Main' , 'St' ] }
>>> objectIDdic[1]
```

The output is shown as follows:

```
['100', 'Main', 'St']
```

Dictionaries are very valuable for reading in feature classes and easily parsing through the data by calling only the rows of interest, among other operations. They are great for ordering and reordering data for use later in a script, so be sure to pay attention to them moving forward.

Iterable data types

Lists, tuples, and strings are all iterable data types that can be used in for loops. When entered into a for loop, these data types are operated on in order, unless otherwise specified. For lists and tuples, this is easy to understand, as they have an obvious order:

```
>>> aList = [1,3,5,7]
>>> for value in aList:
    print value * 2
```

The output is shown as follows:

```
2
6
10
14
```

For strings, each character is looped:

```
>>> aString = "esri"
>>> for value in aString:
    print value.upper()
```

The output is shown as follows:

```
E
S
R
I
```

Dictionaries are also iterable, but with a specific implementation that will only allow direct access to the keys of the dictionary (which can then be used to access the values). Also, the keys are not returned in a specific order:

```
>>> aDict = {"key1":"value1",
    "key2":"value2"}
>>> for value in aDict:
    print value, aDict[value]
```

The output is shown as follows:

```
key2 value2
key1 value1
```

Other important concepts

The use of Python for programming requires an introduction to a number of concepts that are either unique to Python but required or common programming concepts that will be invoked repeatedly when creating scripts. Included following are a number of these concepts that must be covered to be fluent in Python.

Indentation

Python, unlike most other programming languages, enforces strict rules on indenting lines of code. This concept is derived again from Guido's desire to produce clean, readable code. When creating functions or using for loops, or if/else statements, indentation is required on the succeeding lines of code. If a for loop is included inside an if/else statement, there will be two levels of indentation. Veteran programmers of other languages have complained about the strict nature of Python's indentation. New programmers generally find it to be helpful as it makes it easy to organize code. Note that a lot of programmers new to Python will create an indentation error at some point, so make sure to pay attention to the indentation levels.

Functions

Functions are used to take code that is repeated over and over within a script, or across scripts, and make formal tools out of them. Using the keyword **def**, short for the define function, functions are created with defined inputs and outputs. The idea of a function in computing is that it takes data in one state and converts it into data in another state, without affecting any other part of the script. This can be very valuable to automate a GIS analysis.

Here is an example of a function that returns the square of any number supplied:

```
def square(inVal):
    return inVal ** 2
>>> square(3)
```

The output is shown as follows:

```
9
```

While this of course duplicates a similar function built into the math module, it shows the basics of a function. A function (generally) accepts data, transforms it as needed, and then returns the new state of the data using the return keyword.

Keywords

There are a number of keywords built into Python that should be avoided when naming variables. These include `max`, `min`, `sum`, `return`, `list`, `tuple`, `def`, `del`, `from`, `not`, `in`, `as`, `if`, `else`, `elif`, `or`, `while`, `and`, `with`, among many others. Using these keywords will result in an error.

Namespaces

Namespaces are a logical way to organize variable names when a variable inside a function (a local variable) shares the same name as a variable outside of the function (a global variable). Local variables contained within a function (either in the script or within an imported module) and global variables can share a name as long as they do not share a namespace.

This issue often arises when a variable within an imported module unexpectedly has the same name of a variable in the script. Python Interpreter will use namespace rules to decide which variable has been called, which can lead to undesirable results.

Zero-based indexing

As mentioned in the preceding section that describes lists and tuples, Python indexing and counting starts at zero, instead of one. This means that the first member of a group of data is at the zero position, and the second member is at the first position, and so on till the last position.

This rule also applies when there is a for loop iteration within a script. When the iteration starts, the first member of the data being iterated is in the zero position.

Also, indexing can be performed when counting from the last member of an iterable object. In this case, the index of the last member is -1, and the second to last is -2, and so on back to the first member of the object.

Important Python Modules for GIS Analysis

Modules, or code libraries that can be called by a script to increase its programming potential, are either built into Python or are created by third parties and added later to Python. Most of these are written in Python, but a number of them are also written in other programming languages and then wrapped in Python to make them available within Python scripts. Modules are also used to make other programs available to Python, such as the tools built in Microsoft Word.

The ArcPy module

The ArcPy module is both a wrapper module used to interact with the ArcGIS tools, which are then executed by ArcGIS in its internal code format, and a code base that allows for additional control of geospatial analyses and map production. ArcPy is used to control the tools in ArcToolbox, but the tools have not been rewritten in Python; instead, we are able to use the ArcGIS tools using ArcPy. ArcPy also gives us the ability to control ArcGIS Map Documents(MXDs) and the objects that MXDs include: legends, titles, images, layers, and the map view itself. ArcPy also has tools that are not available in ArcToolbox. The most powerful of these are the data cursors, especially the new Data Analysis Cursors that create a more Pythonic interface with GIS data. The data cursors, covered extensively in *Chapters 5, ArcPy Cursors: Search, Insert and Update* and *Chapter 6, Working with ArcPy Geometry Objects* are very useful to extract rows of data from data sources for analysis.

The ability to control geospatial analyses using ArcPy allows for the integration of ArcGIS tools into workflows that contain other powerful Python modules. Python's glue language abilities increase the usefulness of ArcGIS by reducing the need to treat geospatial data in a special manner.

The Operating System (OS) module

The OS module, part of the standard library, allows Python to access operating system functionality. A common use of the module is to use the os.path method to control file paths by dividing them into directory paths (that is, folders) and base paths (that is, files). There is also a useful method, os.walk, which will walk-through a directory and return all files within the folders and subfolders. The OS module is accessed constantly when performing GIS analysis.

The Python System (SYS) module

The sys module, part of the standard library, refers to the Python installation itself. It has a number of methods that will get information about the version of Python installed, as well as information about the script and any arguments (or parameters) supplied to the script, using the sys.argv method. The sys.path method is very useful to append the Python file path; practically, this means that folders containing scripts can be referenced by other scripts to make the functions they contain importable to other scripts.

The XLRD and XLWT modules

The XLRD and XLWT modules are used to read and write Excel spreadsheets, respectively. The modules can be very useful to extract data from legacy spreadsheets and convert them into usable data for GIS analysis, or to write analysis results when a geospatial analysis is completed. They are not part of the Python standard library, but are installed along with ArcGIS 10.2 and Python 2.7.

Commonly used built-in functions

There are a number of built-in functions that we will use throughout the book. The main ones are listed as follows:

- `str`: The string function is used to convert any other type of data into a string
- `int`: The integer function is used to convert a string or float into an integer. To not create an error, any string passed to the integer function must be a number such as 1.
- `float`: The float function is used to convert a string or an integer into a float, much like the integer function.

Commonly used standard library modules

The following standard library modules must be imported:

- `datetime`: The datetime module is used to get information about the date and time, and convert string dates into Python dates.
- `math`: The math module is used for higher level math functions that are necessary at times, such as getting a value for Pi or calculating the square of a number.
- `string`: The string module is used for string manipulations.
- `csv`: The CSV module is used to create and edit comma-separated value type files.

Check out `https://docs.python.org/2/library` for a complete list of the built-in modules in the standard library.

Summary

In this chapter, we discussed about the Zen of Python and covered the basics of programming using Python. We began our exploration of ArcPy and how it can be integrated with other Python modules to produce complete workflows. We also discussed the Python standard library and the basic data types of Python.

Next, we will discuss how to configure Python for use with ArcGIS, and explore how to use Integrated Development Environments (IDEs) to write scripts.

2
Configuring the Python Environment

In this chapter, we will configure both Python and our computer to work together to execute Python scripts. Path variables and environment variables will be configured to ensure that import statements work as expected, and that scripts run when they are clicked on. The structure of the Python folder will be discussed, as will the location of the ArcPy module within the ArcGIS folder structure. We will also discuss **Integrated Development Environments (IDEs)**, programs designed to assist in code creation and code execution, and compare and contrast existing IDEs to determine what benefits each IDE can offer when scripting Python code.

This chapter will cover:

- The location of the Python interpreter, and how it is called to execute a script
- Adjusting the computer's environment variables to ensure correct code execution
- Integrated Development Environments
- Python's folder structure, with a focus on where modules are stored

What is a Python script?

Let's start with the very basics of writing and executing a Python script. What is a Python script? It is a simple text file that contains a series of organized commands written in a formalized language. The text file has the extension .py, but other than that, there is nothing to distinguish it from any other text file. It can be opened using a text editor such as Notepad or Wordpad, but the magic that is Python does not reside in a Python script. Without the Python interpreter, a Python script cannot be run and the commands it contains cannot be executed.

How Python executes a script

Understanding how Python works to interpret a script and then execute the commands within is as important as understanding the Python language itself. Hours of debugging and error checking can be avoided by taking the time to set up Python correctly. The interpretive nature of Python means that a script will have to be first converted into bytecode before it can be executed. We will cover the steps that Python takes to achieve our goal of automating GIS analysis.

What is the Python interpreter?

The Python interpreter, on a Windows environment, is a program that has been compiled into a Windows executable, which has the extension .exe. The Python interpreter, python.exe, has been written in C, an older and extensively used programming language with a more difficult syntax.

Programs written in C, which are also initially written as text files, must be converted into executables by a compiler, a specialized program that converts the text commands into machine code to create executable programs. This is a slow process that can make producing simple programs in C a laborious process. The benefit is that the programs produced are standalone programs capable of running without any dependencies. Python, on the other hand, interprets and executes the Python commands quickly, which makes it a great scripting language, but the scripts must be run through an interpreter and cannot be executed by themselves.

The Python interpreter, as its name implies, interprets commands contained within a Python script. When a Python script is run, or executed, the syntax is first checked to make sure that it conforms to the rules of Python (for example, indentation rules are followed and the variables follow naming conventions). Then, if the script is valid, the commands contained within are converted into bytecode, a specialized code that is executed by the bytecode interpreter, a virtual machine written in C. The bytecode interpreter further converts the bytecode (which is contained within files that end with the extension .pyc) into the correct machine code for the computer being used, and then the CPU executes the script. This is a complex process, which allows Python to maintain a semblance of simplicity.

There are other versions of the Python interpreter that have been written in Java (known as Jython) and in .NET (known as IronPython); these variants are used to write Python scripts in other computing environments and will not be addressed in this book. The ArcGIS installer includes the standard implementation of Python, which is also called CPython to distinguish it from these variants.

Where is the Python interpreter located?

The location of the Python interpreter within the folder structure of a computer is an important detail to master. Python is often downloaded directly from www.python. org and installed separately from ArcGIS. However, each ArcGIS version will require a specific version of Python; given this requirement, the inclusion of Python within the ArcGIS installation package is helpful. For this book, we will be using ArcGIS 10.2, and this will require Python 2.7.

On a Windows machine, the Python folder structure is placed directly on the C: drive, unless it is explicitly loaded on another drive. The installation process for ArcGIS 10.2 will create a folder at C:\Python27, which will contain another folder called either ArcGIS10.2 or ArcGIS10.2x64, depending on the operating system and the version of ArcGIS that has been installed. For this book, I will be using the 32-bit version of ArcGIS, so the final folder path will be at C:\Python27\ArcGIS10.2.

Within this folder are a number of subfolders, as well as python.exe (the Python interpreter). Also included is a second version of the interpreter called pythonw. exe. Pythonw.exe will execute a script without a terminal window with program feedback appearing. Both python.exe and pythonw.exe contain complete copies of all Python commands and can be used to execute a script.

Which Python interpreter should be used?

The general rule to execute a script directly using the Python interpreters is to use pythonw.exe, as no terminal window will appear. When there is a need to test code snippets, or to see the output within a terminal window, start python.exe by double-clicking on the executable.

When python.exe is started, a Python interpreter console will appear:

Note the distinctive three chevrons (**>>>**) that appear below the header explaining version information. That is the Python prompt, where code is entered to be executed line by line, instead of in a completed script. This direct access to the interpreter is useful to test code snippets and understand syntax. A version of this interpreter, the Python Window, has been built into ArcMap and ArcCatalog since ArcGIS 10. It will be discussed more in later chapters.

How does the computer know where the interpreter is?

To be able to execute Python scripts directly (that is, to make the scripts run by double-clicking on them), the computer will also need to know where the interpreter sits within its folder structure. To accomplish this requires both administrative account access and advanced knowledge of how Windows searches for a program. We will have to adjust an environment variable within the advanced system settings dialogue to register the interpreter with the system path.

On a Windows 7 machine, click on the start menu and right-click on **Computer**, then select **Properties** from the menu. On a Windows 8 machine, click on **Windows explorer** and right click on **This PC**, and select **Properties** from the menu. These commands are shortcuts to get to the **Control Panel's System** and **Security/System** menus. Select **Advanced system settings** from the panel on the left. Click on the **Environment Variables** button at the bottom of the **System Properties** menu that appears. In the lower portion of the **Environment Variables** menu, scroll through the **System variables** window until the **Path** variable appears. Select it by clicking on it, and then clicking on the **Edit** button. The following window will appear:

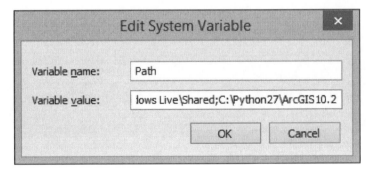

This variable has two components: **Variable name** (path) and **Variable value**. The value is a series of folder paths separated by semicolons. This is the path that is searched when Windows looks for specific executables that have been associated with a file extension. In our case, we will be adding the folder path that contains the Python interpreter. Type C:\Python27\ArcGIS10.2 (or the equivalent on your machine) into the **Variable value** field, making sure to separate it from the value before it with a semicolon. Click on **OK** to exit the **Edit** dialogue, and **OK** to exit the **Environment Variables** menu, and **OK** to exit the **System Properties** menu. The machine will now know where the Python interpreter is, as it will search all folders contained within the Path variable to look for an executable called Python. To test that the path adjustment worked correctly, open up a command window (Start menu/run cmd) and type python. The interpreter should directly run in the command window:

```
C:\Windows\System32\cmd.exe - python                                    _  □  ×

Microsoft Windows [Version 6.3.9600]
(c) 2013 Microsoft Corporation. All rights reserved.

C:\WINDOWS\system32>python
Python 2.7.3 (default, Apr 10 2012, 23:31:26) [MSC v.1500 32 bit (Intel)] on win
32
Type "help", "copyright", "credits" or "license" for more information.
>>> import math
>>>
```

If the Python header with version information and the triple chevron appears, the path adjustment has worked correctly.

> If there is no admin access available, there is a work around. In a command-line window, pass the entire path to the Python interpreter (C:\Python27\ArcGIS10.2\python.exe) to start the interpreter.

Make Python scripts executable when clicked on

The final step in making the scripts run when double-clicked (which also means they can run outside of the ArcGIS environment, saving lots of memory overhead) is to associate files with the .py extension with the Python interpreter. If the scripts have not already been associated with the interpreter, they will appear as files of an unknown type or as a text file.

To change this, right-click on a **Python** script. Select **Open With**, and then select **Choose Default Program**. If python.exe or pythonw.exe does not appear as a choice, navigate to the folder that holds them (C:\Python27\ArcGIS10.2, in this case) and select either python.exe or pythonw.exe. Again, the difference between the two is the appearance of a terminal window when the scripts are run using python.exe, which will contain any output from the script (but this window will disappear when the script is done). I recommend using pythonw.exe when executing scripts, and python.exe to test code.

 Python scripts can also explicitly call pythonw.exe by adjusting the extension to .pyw instead of .py.

Integrated Development Environments (IDEs)

The Python interpreter contains everything that is needed to execute a Python script or to test Python code by interacting with the Python interpreter. However, writing scripts requires a text editor. There are usually at least two simple text editors included on a Windows machine (Notepad and Wordpad) and they work in an emergency to edit a script or even write a whole script. Unfortunately, they are very simple and do not allow the user functionality that would make it easier to write multiple scripts or very long scripts.

To bridge the gap, a series of programs collectively known as Integrated Development Environments have been developed. IDEs exist for all programming languages, and include functions such as variable listing, code assist, and more, that make them ideal to craft programming scripts. We will review a few of them to assess their usefulness to write Python scripts. The three discussed as follows are all free and well-established within different Python communities.

IDLE

Python includes an IDE when it is installed. The IDE is called IDLE, which is a word play on both IDE and the name of a prominent member of Monty Python, Eric Idle. It can be started in Windows 7 by going to the Start menu and finding the ArcGIS folder within the **Programs** menu. Within the Python folder, IDLE will be one of the choices within that folder. Select it to start **IDLE**.

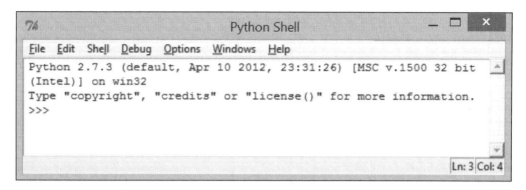

IDLE contains an interactive interpreter (i.e. the triple chevron) and the ability to run complete Python scripts. It is also written using Python's built-in GUI module, called **Tkinter**, so it has the advantage of being written in the same language that it executes.

Another advantage of using IDLE over the Python console (`python.exe`) is that any print statements or other script output is directed to the IDLE interactive window, which does not disappear after executing the script. IDLE is also lightweight with respect to memory use. Scripts are opened using a file dialogue contained within the **File** menu, and recently run scripts are listed within the **File** menu's, **Recent Files**.

Disadvantages of IDLE include a limited code assist (or code auto-complete), a useful IDE tool, and having no way to organize scripts into logical projects. There is no way to find all variables contained within a script, another useful feature of other IDEs. Also, the **Recent Files** menu has a limit on the number of scripts that it will list, making it harder to find a script that has not been run in months (which is a common occurrence, believe me!). IDLE is a passable IDE that is useful if no other programs can be installed on the machine. It is also very useful for rapid testing of code snippets. While it is not my main IDE, I find myself using IDLE almost daily.

PythonWin

PythonWin (short for Python for Windows) is available at `http://sourceforge.net/projects/pywin32/files/pywin32`, and includes both an IDE and helpful modules to use Python in a Windows environment. Select the newest build of **PythonWin**, and then select the correct version 32 module based on the installed version of Python (for my machine, I selected `pywin32-218.win32-py2.7.exe`, the correct version for my 32-bit Python 2.7 installation). Run the executable, and if the correct version has been downloaded, the installation GUI will recognize Python 2.7 in the system registry and will install itself.

PythonWin includes an Interactive Window where the user can directly interact with the Python interpreter. Scripts can also be opened within PythonWin, and it includes a set of tiling commands in the Windows menu that allows the user to organize the display of all open scripts and the Interactive Window.

Another nice advantage that PythonWin has over IDLE is the ability to display different portions of a script within the same script window. If a script has grown too long, it can be a pain to scroll up and down the script when editing. PythonWin allows the user to pull down from the top of the script to create a second script window, which can focus on a separate part of the script. Also, on the left side, another window can be opened that will list Python classes and variables, making it easier to navigate to a particular section of the script.

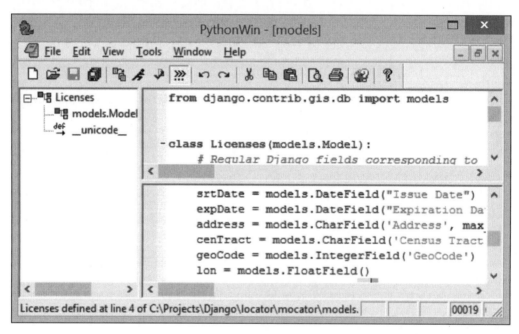

One small but helpful feature built into PythonWin's Interactive Window is the ability to search through previously entered code statements. At the triple chevron prompt, hold down the *Ctrl* key and use the up and down arrow keys to navigate through the lines to find one of interest. This saves a lot of time when testing a particular snippet of code.

All in all, PythonWin is a useful and easy-to-use IDE, and most ArcGIS professionals who create Python scripts use PythonWin. The drawbacks I find with PythonWin include its lack of ability to organize scripts into projects, and its lack of a list of variables that exist within the script, which can be very helpful when navigating larger scripts.

Aptana Studio 3

Sometimes the tools of the greater programming community can seem daunting to new scripters, who are more focused on simply creating a script that will save time on a GIS analysis than using the correct tool for programming daily. It reminds me of inexperienced computer users, who don't feel like they need the full power of a top-of-the-line computer because they only want to browse the internet and send e-mails.

However, the exact opposite is true: the computer adverse is better off having an easier to use top-of-the-line computer, while an experienced computer user could make do with a net book.

The same can be said for programmers and scripters. Sometimes, it's better to have an over-the-top IDE that will actually make a scripter more productive, while an experienced programmer could make do with Notepad. All of the bells and whistles included in an IDE such as Aptana Studio 3 will save scripters time and take remarkably little time to learn.

Aptana Studio 3 is available at `http://aptana.com`. Download and run the installer provided to install it. Choose a default main project folder that can contain all of the scripts projects; for this book, I created a folder called `C:\Projects`. For each project created, Aptana will create a project file holding information about each project. When using Aptana Studio at work, using a network folder can be useful as others can then access the projects with their respective Aptana installations.

Once it has been installed, the next step is to create a `PyDev` project. Go to the **File** menu and select **New**, and then select **PyDev** project. When creating this first project, Python Interpreter will have to be added to Aptana's Python path. Aptana can support more than one interpreter; for our purposes, one will do. Go to the bottom of the PyDev project menu and click on **Click here** to configure an interpreter. When the **Preferences/Python Interpreters** menu appears, make sure to select **Interpreter-Python** on the left, and then click on **New** in the top-right menu.

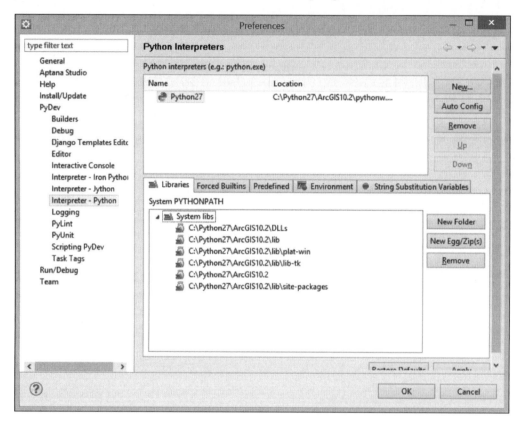

Once **New** has been selected, a small dialog will appear asking for a name for the interpreter and the path to the executable. Click on **browse** and navigate to the folder with `python.exe`. No terminal window will be generated when running a Python script using Aptana Studio as all output is redirected to the Aptana Studio console. Select `python.exe` and click on **OK**. Next, click on **OK** in the **Select Interpreter** menu, and then click on **OK** in the **Preferences** menu. Back in the **PyDev Project** menu, give the project a name, and either use the default workspace location or a custom one (for example, `C:\Projects`).

All of this configuration only has to happen the first time; once that is done, creating a **PyDev** project will only require giving a name and location. Now, all of the scripts associated with that project will always be listed in the left menu (**PyDev Package Explorer**), which is a very powerful way to organize projects and scripts.

Making sure that Aptana Studio is in the PyDev perspective (in the **Windows/Open Perspective/Other** menu, choose **PyDev**) will give three main windows–**Package Explorer** on the left, **Script window** in the middle, and **Outline window** on the right, where variables contained within a script are listed. Clicking on one of the variables on the right will move the script window to that section of the code, making script navigation fast. Also, I like to add the Console window in the middle below the Script window, where the output of the script can be displayed.

Open scripts each have a tab within the Script window, making it easy to switch between the scripts. Also, the windows can be closed to give more room to the Script window as needed. Hovering over a variable within a script will call up a pop-up menu that describes where the variable was first created, which can be a lifesaver as it is easy to forget at times which variable is which (unless, of course, they are clearly named according to the rules described in the previous chapter; even then, it can be a pain at times).

IDE summary

There are many other IDEs, both commercial and free, available for coding in Python. In the end, each GIS analyst must choose the tool that makes them feel productive and comfortable. This may change as programming becomes a bigger part of their daily work flow. Be sure to test out a few different IDEs to find one that is easy to use and intuitive.

Python folder structure

Python's folder structure holds more than just the Python Interpreter. Within the subfolders reside a number of important scripts, digital link libraries, and even C language modules. Not all of the scripts are used all the time, but each has a role in making the Python programming environment possible. The most important folder to know about is the **site-packages** folder, where most modules that will be imported in Python scripts are contained.

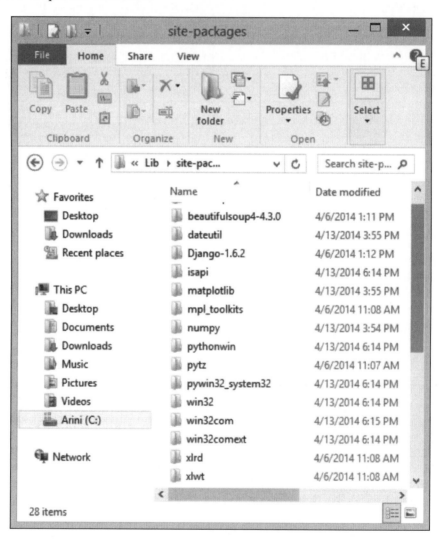

Where modules reside

Within every Python folder is a folder called `Lib`, and within that folder is a folder called `site-packages`. On my machine, the folder sits at `C:\Python27\ArcGIS10.2\Lib\site-packages`. Almost all third-party modules are copied into this folder to be imported as needed. The main exception to this rule, for our purposes, is the ArcPy module, which is stored within the `ArcGIS` folder in the `Program Files` folder (for example, `C:\Program Files (x86)\ArcGIS\Desktop10.2\arcpy`). To make that possible, the ArcGIS installer adjusts the Python system path (using the sys module) to make the arcPy module importable.

Using Python's sys module to add a module

Python's sys module is a module that allows the user to take advantage of system tools built into the Python Interpreter. One of the most useful of the functions in the sys module is `sys.path`. It is a list of file paths, which the user can modify to adjust where Python will look for a module to import, without needing administrative access.

When Python 2.7 is installed by the ArcGIS 10.2 installer, the installer takes advantage of the `sys.path` functions to add `C:\Program Files (x86)\ArcGIS\Desktop10.2\arcpy` to the system path. To test this, start the Python Interpreter or an IDE and type the following:

```
>>> import sys
>>> print sys.path
```

The output is as follows:

```
['', 'C:\\WINDOWS\\SYSTEM32\\python27.zip', 'C:\\Python27\\ArcGIS10.2\\
Dlls', 'C:\\Python27\\ArcGIS10.2\\lib', 'C:\\Python27\\ArcGIS10.2\\lib\\
plat-win', 'C:\\Python27\\ArcGIS10.2\\lib\\lib-tk', 'C:\\Python27\\
ArcGIS10.2\\Lib\\site-packages\\pythonwin', 'C:\\Python27\\ArcGIS10.2',
'C:\\Python27\\ArcGIS10.2\\lib\\site-packages', 'C:\\Program Files
(x86)\\ArcGIS\\Desktop10.2\\bin', 'C:\\Program Files (x86)\\ArcGIS\\
Desktop10.2\\arcpy', 'C:\\Program Files (x86)\\ArcGIS\\Desktop10.2\\
ArcToolbox\\Scripts', 'C:\\Python27\\ArcGIS10.2\\lib\\site-packages\\
win32', 'C:\\Python27\\ArcGIS10.2\\lib\\site-packages\\win32\\lib']
```

The system path (stored in the variable `sys.path`) includes all of the folders that ArcPy requires to automate ArcGIS. The system path incorporates all directories listed in the PYTHONPATH environment variable (if one has been created); this is separate from the Windows path environment variable discussed previously. The two separate path variables work together to help Python locate modules.

The sys.path.append() method

The `sys.path` function is a list (did you notice the square brackets in the preceding code output?) and as such can be appended or extended to include new file paths that will point to modules the user wants to import. To avoid the need to adjust `sys.path`, copy the module into the site-packages folder. When this is not possible, use the `sys.path.append()` method instead:

```
>>> sys.path.append("C:\\Projects\\Requests")
>>> sys.path
['', 'C:\\WINDOWS\\SYSTEM32\\python27.zip',
 'C:\\Python27\\ArcGIS10.2\\Dells',
 'C:\\Python27\\ArcGIS10.2\\lib',
..'C:\\Python27\\ArcGIS10.2\\lib\\plat-win',
..'C:\\Python27\\ArcGIS10.2\\lib\\lib-tk',
..'C:\\Python27\\ArcGIS10.2\\Lib\\site-packages\\pythonwin',
..'C:\\Python27\\ArcGIS10.2',
..'C:\\Python27\\ArcGIS10.2\\lib\\site-packages', 'C:\\Program
..Files (x86)\\ArcGIS\\Desktop10.2\\bin', 'C:\\Program Files
..(x86)\\ArcGIS\\Desktop10.2\\arcpy', 'C:\\Program Files
..(x86)\\ArcGIS\\Desktop10.2\\ArcToolbox\\Scripts',
..'C:\\Python27\\ArcGIS10.2\\lib\\site-packages\\win32',
..'C:\\Python27\\ArcGIS10.2\\lib\\site-packages\\win32\\lib',
..'C:\\Projects\\Requests']
```

When the `sys.path.append()` method is used, the adjustment is temporary. Adjust the PYTHONPATH environment variable in the **Windows System Properties** menu (discussed in the path environment variable section) to make a permanent change (and create the PYTHONPATH if it has not been created).

One last note is that to import a module without adjusting the system path or copying the module into the site-packages folder, place the module in the folder with the script that is importing it. As long as the module is configured correctly, it will work normally. This is useful when there is no administrative access available to a machine.

Summary

In this chapter, we covered a lot about how Python works to execute scripts and commands, and about development environments used to craft scripts. In particular, we discussed how a Python script is read and executed by the Python Interpreter, where the Python Interpreter is located within the Python folder structure, and what the different Python script extensions mean (`.py`, `.pyc`, `.pyw`). We also covered Integrated Development Environments and how they compare and contrast.

In the next chapter, we will cover how to use ModelBuilder to convert a modeled analysis into a Python script, and how to make it more powerful than the exported version.

3
Creating the First Python Script

Now that we have Python configured to fit our needs, we can create Python scripts. This chapter will explore how to use ArcGIS **ModelBuilder** to model a simple analysis as the basis for our script. ModelBuilder is very useful on its own and for creating Python scripts as it has an operational and a visual component, and all models can be outputted as Python scripts. This will allow us to compare how the more familiar ModelBuilder utilizes tools in the ArcToolbox to how Python handles the same tools. We will also discuss iteration and when it is best to use Python over ModelBuilder.

In this chapter, we will cover the following topics:

- Modeling a simple analysis using ModelBuilder
- Exporting the model out to a Python script

Prerequisites

"Along with ArcGIS ModelBuilder, a data set and scripts are required."

For this chapter, the accompanying data and scripts should be downloaded from Packt Publishing's website. The completed scripts are available for comparison purposes and the data will be used for this chapter's analysis.

ModelBuilder

ArcGIS has been in development since the 1970s. During that time, it included a variety of programming languages and tools to help GIS analysts automate analyses and map production. These include the Avenue scripting language in the ArcGIS 3x series and the **ARC Macro Language** (**AML**) in the ARC/Info workstation days, as well as VBScript up until ArcGIS 10x when Python was introduced. Another useful tool introduced in ArcGIS 9x was ModelBuilder, a visual programming environment used for both modeling analysis and creating tools that can be used repeatedly with different input feature classes.

Another useful feature of ModelBuilder is an export function that allows modelers to create Python scripts directly from a model. This will make it easier to compare how inputs in a ModelBuilder tool are accepted versus how a Python script calls the same tool and supplies the inputs to it, or how the feature classes that are created are named and placed within the file structure. ModelBuilder is a fantastic tool that will make it easy for a GIS analyst to bridge the gap from normal GIS workflows to automated Python-based workflows.

Creating a model and exporting to Python

This chapter will depend on the downloadable SanFrancisco.gdb file geodatabase, available from the Packt Publishing website. The San Francisco GDB contains data downloaded from data.sfgov.org and the US Census' American Factfinder website available at factfinder2.census.gov. All census and geographic data included in the geodatabase is from the 2010 census. The data is contained within a feature dataset called **SanFrancisco**. The data in this feature dataset is in NAD 83 California State Plane Zone 3 and the linear unit of measure is the US Foot (this corresponds to SRID 2227 in the European Petroleum Survey Group, or EPSG, format).

The analysis we will create with the model, and eventually export to Python for further refinement, will use bus stops along a specific line in San Francisco. These bus stops will be buffered to create a representative region around each bus stop. The buffered areas will then be intersected with census blocks to find out how many people are within each representative region around the bus stops.

Modeling the Select and Buffer tools

Using ModelBuilder, we will first model the basis of the bus stop analysis. Once it has been modeled, it will be exported as an automatically generated Python script. Follow these steps to begin the analysis:

1. Open up **ArcCatalog** and create a folder connection to the folder containing `SanFrancisco.gdb`. Right-click on geodatabase and add a new toolbox called **Chapter3Tools**.

2. Next, open **ModelBuilder** and create a Model, saving it in the **Chapter3Tools** toolbox as **Chapter3Model1.**

3. Drag the **Bus_Stops** feature class and the **Select** tool from the **Analysis/ Extract** toolset in **ArcToolbox**.

4. Open the **Select** tool and name the output feature class `Inbound71`. Make sure that the feature class is written to the **Chapter3Results** feature dataset into the model.

5. Open the **Expression** SQL Query Builder and create the following SQL expression: **NAME = '71 IB' AND BUS_SIGNAG = 'Ferry Plaza'**.

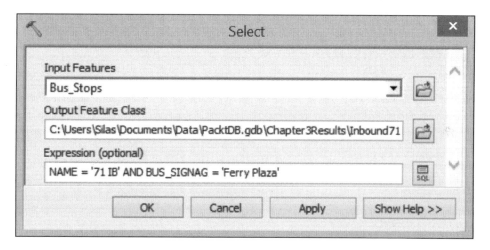

6. The next step is to add a **Buffer** tool from the **Analysis/Proximity** toolset. The **Buffer** tool will be used to create buffers around each bus stop. The buffered bus stops allow us to intersect with census data in the form of census blocks, creating the representative regions around each bus stop.

7. Connect the output of the **Select** tool (**Inbound71**) to the **Buffer** tool. Open up the **Buffer** tool and add 400 to the **Distance** field, and make the units **Feet**. Leave the rest of the options blank. Click on **OK** and return to the model.

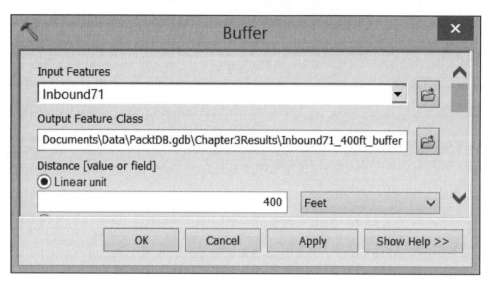

Adding the Intersect tool

Now that we have selected the bus line of interest, and buffered the stops to create representative regions, we will need to intersect the regions with the census blocks to find the population of each representative region:

1. First, add the **CensusBlocks2010** feature class from the **SanFrancisco** feature dataset to the model.

2. Next, add the **Intersect** tool, located in the **Analysis/Overlay** toolset in **ArcToolbox**. While we could use **Spatial Join** to achieve a similar result, I am using the **Intersect** tool to capture the area of intersect for use later in the model and script.

At this point, our model should look like this:

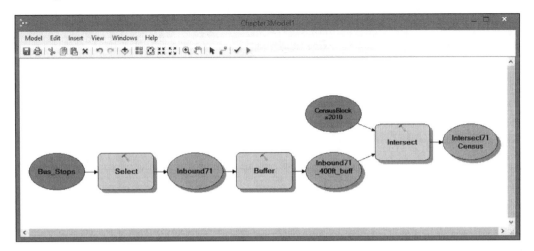

Tallying the analysis results

After we created this simple analysis, the next step is to determine the results for each bus stop. Finding the number of people that live in census blocks touched by the 400 feet buffer of each bus stop involves examining each row of data in the final feature class and selecting rows that correspond to the bus stop. Once these are selected, a sum of the selected rows would be calculated either using the **Field Calculator** or the **Summarize** tool. All of these methods will work, and yet none are perfect. They take too long, and worse, are not repeatable automatically if an assumption in the model is adjusted (if the buffer is adjusted from 400 feet to 500 feet, for instance).

This is where the traditional uses of ModelBuilder begin to fail analysts. It should be easy to instruct the model to select all rows associated with each bus stop, and then generate a summed population figure for each bus stop's representative region. It would be even better to have the model create a spreadsheet to contain the final results of the analysis. It's time to use Python to take this analysis to the next level.

Exporting the model and adjusting the script

While modeling analysis in ModelBuilder has its drawbacks, there is one fantastic option built into ModelBuilder; the ability to create a model and then export the model to Python. Along with the ArcGIS help documentation, it is the best way to discover the correct Python syntax to use when writing ArcPy scripts.

Create a folder that can hold the exported scripts next to the **SanFrancisco** geodatabase (for example, C:\Projects\Scripts). This will hold both the exported scripts that ArcGIS automatically generates, and the versions that we will build from those generated scripts.

Open the model called **Chapter3Model1** and click on the **Model** menu in the upper left. Select **Export** from the menu, and then select **To Python Script**. Save the script in the script folder as Chapter3Model1.py.

> Note that there is also the option to export the model as a graphic. Creating a graphic of the model is a good way to share what the model is doing with other analysts without the need to share the model and the data, and can also be useful when sharing Python scripts as well.

The automatically generated script

Open the automatically generated script in an IDE. It should look like this:

```
# -*- coding: utf-8 -*-

# ----------------------------------------------------------------
----

# 8662_Chapter3Model1.py

# Created on: 2014-04-22 21:59:31.00000

#    (generated by ArcGIS/ModelBuilder)

# Description:

# ----------------------------------------------------------------
----

# Import arcpy module

import arcpy
```

```
# Local variables:

Bus_Stops = "C:\\Projects\\PacktDB.gdb\\SanFrancisco\\Bus_Stops"

CensusBlocks2010 = "C:\\Projects\\PacktDB.gdb\\SanFrancisco\\
CensusBlocks2010"

Inbound71 = "C:\\Projects\\PacktDB.gdb\\Chapter3Results\\Inbound71"

Inbound71_400ft_buffer = "C:\\Projects\\PacktDB.gdb\\Chapter3Results\\
Inbound71_400ft_buffer"

Intersect71Census = "C:\\Projects\\PacktDB.gdb\\Chapter3Results\\
Intersect71Census"

# Process: Select

arcpy.Select_analysis(Bus_Stops,

                      Inbound71,

                      "NAME = '71 IB' AND BUS_SIGNAG = 'Ferry Plaza'")

# Process: Buffer

arcpy.Buffer_analysis(Inbound71,

                      Inbound71_400ft_buffer,

                      "400 Feet", "FULL", "ROUND", "NONE", "")

# Process: Intersect

arcpy.Intersect_analysis("C:\\Projects\\PacktDB.gdb\\Chapter3Results\\
Inbound71_400ft_buffer #;C:\\Projects\\PacktDB.gdb\\SanFrancisco\\
CensusBlocks2010 #", Intersect71Census, "ALL", "", "INPUT")
```

Let's examine this script line by line. The first line is preceded by a pound sign (#), which again means that this line is a comment; however, it is not ignored by the Python interpreter when the script is executed as usual but is used to help Python interpret the encoding of the script as described here: http://legacy.python.org/dev/peps/pep-0263.

The second commented line and the third line are included for decorative purposes. The next four lines, all commented, are used to provide readers with information about the script, what it is called and when it was created, along with a description that is pulled from the model's properties. Another decorative line is included to separate out the informative header from the body of the script visually. While the commented information section is nice to include in a script for other users of the script, it is not necessary.

The body of the script, or the executable portion of the script, starts with the `import arcpy` line. Import statements are, by convention, included at the top of the body of the script. In this instance, the only module that is being imported is ArcPy.

ModelBuilder's export function creates not only an executable script, but also comments each section to help mark the different sections of the script. The comments let the user know where the variables are located and where the ArcToolbox tools are being executed. The comments will grow to be superfluous as the reader grows to understand the code, but it was nice of ESRI to include the comments.

Below the import statements are the variables. In this case, the variables represent the file paths to the input and output feature classes. The variable names are derived from the names of the feature classes (the base names of the file paths). The file paths are assigned to the variables using the assignment operator (=), and the parts of the file paths are separated by two backslashes.

File paths in Python

It would be good to review how file paths are used in Python compared to how they are represented in Windows. In Python, file paths are strings, and strings in Python have special characters used to represent tabs (\t), newlines (\n), or carriage returns (\r), among many others. These special characters all incorporate single backslashes, making it very hard to create a file path that uses single backslashes. This would not be a big deal, except that file paths in Windows Explorer all use single backslashes.

There are a number of methods used to avoid this issue. Python was developed within the Linux environment, where file paths have forward slashes. This more Pythonic representation is also available when using Python in a Windows environment, demonstrated as follows:

```
Windows Explorer:  "C:\Projects\PacktDB.gdb\Chapter3Results\
Intersect71Census"
Pythonic version:   "C:/Projects/PacktDB.gdb/Chapter3Results/
Intersect71Census"
```

Within a Python script, the file path with the forward slashes will work, while the Windows Explorer version might cause the script to throw an exception.

Another method used to avoid the issue with special characters is the one employed by ModelBuilder when it automatically creates the Python scripts from a model. In this case, the backslashes are escaped using a second backslash. The preceding script uses this second method to produce the following results:

```
Python escaped version:  "C:\\Projects\\PacktDB.gdb\\Chapter3Results\\
Intersect71Census"
```

The third method, which I prefer, is to create what is known as a raw string. This is the same as a regular string, but it includes an **r** before the script begins. This r alerts the Python Interpreter that the following script does not contain any special characters or escape characters. Here is an example of how it is used:

```
Python raw string:  r"C:\Projects\PacktDB.gdb\Chapter3Results\
Intersect71Census"
```

Using raw strings will make it easier to grab a file path from Windows Explorer and add it to a string inside a script. It will also make it easier to avoid accidentally forgetting to include a set of double backslashes in a file path, which happens all the time and is the cause of many script bugs.

Continuing the script analysis: the ArcPy tools

The next, and most important, section of the script is where the analysis is executed. The same tools that we created in the model, the **Select**, the **Buffer**, and the **Intersect** tools, are included in this section. The same parameters that we supplied in the model are also included here: the inputs and outputs, plus the SQL statement in the Select tool, and the buffer distance in the **Buffer** tool.

The tool parameters are supplied to the tools in the script in the same order as they appear in the tool interfaces in the model. Here is the **Select** tool in the script:

```
arcpy.Select_analysis(Bus_Stops, Inbound71, "NAME = '71 IB' AND BUS_
SIGNAG = 'Ferry Plaza'")
```

It works like this. The arcPy module has a method, or a special property, called `Select_analysis`. This method, when called, requires three parameters: the input feature class (or shapefile), the output feature class, and the SQL statement. In this example, the input is represented by the variable `Bus_Stops` and the output feature class is represented by the variable `Inbound71`, both of which are defined in the variable section. The SQL statement is included as the third parameter. Note that it could also be represented by a variable, if the variable was defined above this line; the SQL statement, as a string, could be assigned to a variable and the variable could replace the SQL statement as the third parameter. Here is an example of parameter replacement using a variable:

```
sqlStatement = "NAME = '71 IB' AND BUS_SIGNAG = 'Ferry Plaza'"
arcpy.Select_analysis(Bus_Stops, Inbound71, sqlStatement)
```

While ModelBuilder is good about assigning input and output feature classes to variables, it does not assign variables to every portion of the parameter. This will be an important thing to correct when we adjust and build our own scripts.

The **Buffer** tool accepts a similar set of parameters as the **Select** tool. There is an input feature class represented by a variable, an output feature class variable, and the distance that we provided (400 feet in this case), along with a series of parameters that are supplied by default. Note that the parameters rely on keywords, and these key words can be adjusted within the text of the script to adjust the resulting buffer output. For instance, Feet could be adjusted to Meters and the buffer would much larger. Check the help section of the tool to better understand how the other parameters will affect the buffer and to find the key words arguments that will be accepted by the **Buffer** tool in ArcPy. Also, as noted earlier, all of the parameters could be assigned to variables, which can save time if the same parameters are used repeatedly throughout a script.

Sometimes the supplied parameter is merely an empty string, as is the case here with the last parameter:

```
arcpy.Buffer_analysis(Inbound71,Inbound71_400ft_buffer,
                    "400 Feet", "FULL", "ROUND", "NONE", "")
```

The empty string, which in this case signifies that there is not a dissolve field for this buffer, is found quite frequently within ArcPy. It could also be represented by two single quotes, but ModelBuilder has been built to use double quotes to encase strings.

The Intersect tool and string manipulation

The last tool, the Intersect tool, uses a different method to represent the files that need to be intersected together when the tool is executed. Because the tool accepts multiple files in the input section (meaning there is no limit to the number of files that can be intersected together in one operation), it stores all of the file paths within one string. The string uses the hash or pound sign (#) to separate the file paths within the input string. This slight deviation must be dealt with if we are to use the Intersect tool in a Script tool. If we are building a tool from this script, we will not know the files that will be intersected before they are run, so we need to know the methods to deal with inserting variables into strings.

There are three methods to insert variables into strings. Each method has different advantages and disadvantages of a technical nature. It's good to know about all three of them as they have uses beyond our needs here, so let's review them.

The string manipulation method 1–string addition

String addition is an odd concept at first as it would not seem possible to add strings together, unlike integers or floats, which are numbers. However, within Python and other programming languages, this is a normal step. Using the plus sign (+), strings are added together to make longer strings or allow variables to be added to the middle of existing strings. Here are some examples of this process:

```
>>> aString = "This is a string"
>>> bString = " and this is another string"
>>> aString + bString
```

The output is as follows:

```
'This is a string and this is another string'
```

```
>>> cString = aString + bString
>>> cString
```

The output is as follows:

```
'This is a string and this is another string'
```

Two or more strings can be added together, and can even be assigned to a third variable. This process can be useful for situations such as the input string for the Intersect tool. The string can be broken up and variables representing the file paths can be inserted into the middle of the string:

```
filePath1 = r"C:\Projects\Inbound71_400ft_buffer"
filePath2 =  r"C:\Projects\CensusBlocks2010"
arcpy.Intersect_analysis(filePath1 + " #;" + filePath2 + " #",
Intersect71Census, "ALL", "", "INPUT")
```

This is a powerful and useful way to insert the file paths into the input string. As long as the separators are still included in the string, the string will still be valid and the Intersect tool will run as expected. Here is what the string will look like when the string addition is completed:

```
>>> filePath1 = r"C:\Projects\Inbound71_400ft_buffer"
>>> filePath2 =  r"C:\Projects\CensusBlocks2010"
>>> inputString = filePath1 + " #;" + filePath2 + " #"
>>> print inputString
```

The output is as follows:

```
C:\Projects\Inbound71_400ft_buffer #;C:\Projects\CensusBlocks2010 #
```

Another similar offshoot of string addition is string multiplication, where strings are multiplied by an integer to produce repeated versions of the string:

```
>>>"string" * 3
```

The output is as follows:

```
'stringstringstring'
```

The string manipulation method 2–string formatting #1

The second method of string manipulation, known as string formatting, involves adding placeholders into the string that will accept specific kinds of data. This means that these special strings can accept other strings as well as integers and float values. These placeholders use the modulo (%) and a key letter to indicate the type of data to expect. Strings are represented using **%s**, floats are represented using **%f**, and integers are represented using **%d**. The floats can also be adjusted to limit the digits included by adding a modifying number after the modulo. If there is more than one placeholder in a string, the values are passed to the string in a tuple.

This method has become less popular since the third method discussed in the following section was introduced in Python 2.6, but it is still valuable to know as many older scripts use it. Here is an example of this method:

```
>>> origString = "This string has as a placeholder %s"
>>> newString = origString % "and this text was added"
>>> print newString
```

The output is as follows:

```
This string has as a placeholder and this text was added
```

Here is an example when using a float placeholder:

```
>>> floatString1 = "This string has a float here: %f"
>>> newString = floatString1 % 1.0
>>> print newString
```

The output is as follows:

```
This string has a float here: 1.000000
>>> floatString2 = "This string has a float here: %.1f"
```

```
>>> newString2 = floatString2 % 1.0
>>> print newString2
```

The output is as follows:

```
This string has a float here: 1.0
```

Here is an example using an integer placeholder:

```
>>> intString = "Here is an integer: %d"
>>> newString = intString % 1
>>> print newString
```

The output is as follows:

```
Here is an integer: 1
```

For the **Intersect** tool, the %s symbol can be used to accept the file path string variables:

```
filePath1 = r"C:\Projects\Inbound71_400ft_buffer"
filePath2 =  r"C:\Projects\CensusBlocks2010"
arcpy.Intersect_analysis("%s #;%s #" % (filePath1,filePath2),
Intersect71Census, "ALL", "", "INPUT")
```

The string manipulation method 3–string formatting #2

The final method, the most recently introduced, is also known as string formatting. It is similar to the string formatting discussed earlier, with the added benefit of not requiring a specific type of placeholder. The placeholders, or tokens as they are also known, are only required to be in order to be accepted. The format function is built into strings; by adding `.format` to the string, and passing in parameters, the string accepts the values:

```
>>> formatString = "This string has 3 tokens: {0}, {1}, {2}"
>>> newString = formatString.format("String", 2.5, 4)
>>> print newString
```

```
The output is as follows:
```

```
This string has 3 tokens: String, 2.5, 4
```

The tokens don't have to be in order within the string, and can even be repeated. The order is derived from the parameters supplied to the `.format` function that passes the values to the string.

For the **Intersect** tool, the string formatting would look like this:

```
filePath1 = r"C:\Projects\Inbound71_400ft_buffer"

filePath2 =  r"C:\Projects\CensusBlocks2010"

arcpy.Intersect_analysis("{0} #;{1} #".format(filePath1,filePath2),
Intersect71Census, "ALL", "", "INPUT")
```

The third method has become my go-to method for string manipulation because of the ability to add the values repeatedly and make it possible to avoid supplying the wrong type of data to a specific placeholder, unlike the second method.

Adjusting the Script

Now is the time to take the automatically generated script and adjust it to fit our needs. We want the script to both produce the output data, and to have it analyze the data and tally the results into a spreadsheet. This spreadsheet will hold an averaged population value for each bus stop. The average will be derived from each census block that the buffered representative region surrounding the stops intersected. Save the original script as Chapter3Model1Modified.py.

Adding the CSV module to the script

For this script, we will use the **CSV** module, a useful module to create Comma Separated Value spreadsheets. Its simple syntax will make it a useful tool to create script outputs. It should be noted that ArcGIS for Desktop also installs the **xlrd** and **xlwt** modules, used to read or generate Excel spreadsheets respectively, when it is installed.

Just below the import arcPy line, add import csv. This will allow us to use the csv module to create the spreadsheet:

```
# Import arcpy module
import arcpy
import csv
```

The next adjustment is made to the **Intersect** tool. Notice that the two paths included in the input string are also defined as variables in the variable section. Remove the file paths from the input strings and replace them with numbered placeholder tokens, and then add the format function and supply the variables as placeholders:

```
# Process: Intersect
arcpy.Intersect_analysis("{0} #;{1}#".format( .............
Inbound71_400ft_buffer,CensusBlocks2010),
                        Intersect71Census, "ALL", "", "INPUT")
```

Accessing the data: Using a cursor

Now that the script is in place to generate the raw data we need, we need a way to access the data held in the output feature class from the **Intersect** tool. This access will allow us to aggregate the rows of data representing each bus stop. We also need something to hold the aggregate data in the memory, to be written to the spreadsheet.

To accomplish the second part, we will use a Python dictionary. To accomplish the first part, we will use a method built into the ArcPy module: the Data Access Search Cursor.

The Python dictionary will be added below the **Intersect** tool. A dictionary in Python is created using curly brackets. Add the following line to the script:

dataDictionary = {}

This script will use the Bus Stop IDs as keys for the dictionary. The values will be lists, which will hold all of the population values associated with each Bus Stop ID. Add the following lines to generate a Data Cursor:

```
with arcpy.da.SearchCursor(Intersect71Census, ["STOPID","POP10"]) as
cursor:
    for row in cursor:
        busStopID = row[0]
        pop10 = row[1]
        if busStopID not in dataDictionary.keys():
            dataDictionary[busStopID] = [pop10]
        else:
            dataDictionary[busStopID].append(pop10)
```

This iteration combines a few ideas in Python and ArcPy. The with … as statement is used to create a variable (cursor) that represents the `arcpy.da.SearchCursor` object. It could also be written like this:

```
cursor = arcpy.da.SearchCursor(Intersect71Census, ["STOPID","POP10"])
```

The advantage of the with ... as structure is that the cursor object is erased from memory when the iteration is completed, which eliminates locks on the feature classes being evaluated.

The `arcpy.da.SearchCursor()` function requires an input feature class, and a list of fields to be returned. Optionally, a SQL statement can limit the number of rows returned.

The next line, `for row in cursor`, is the iteration through the data. It is not a normal Pythonic iteration, a distinction that will have ramifications in certain instances. For instance, however, it does allow for row-by-row access to data contained within the supplied feature class. Note that when using a Search Cursor, each row of data is returned as a tuple, which cannot be modified. The data can be accessed using indexes, as shown in the preceding code, where the two members of the tuple are assigned to variables.

The if/else conditional allows the data to be sorted. As noted earlier, the Bus Stop IDs, which are the first member of the data included in the tuple, will be used as a key. The conditional evaluates whether the Bus Stop ID is included in the dictionary's existing keys (which are contained in a list and accessed using the `dictionary.keys()` method). If it is not, it is added to the keys, and assigned a value that is a list containing (at first) one piece of data, the population value contained in that row. If it does exist in the keys, the list is appended with the next population value associated with that Bus Stop ID. With this code, we have now sorted each census block population according to the Bus Stop with which it is associated.

Next, we need to add code to create the spreadsheet. This code will use the same with ... as structure, and will generate an average population value by using two built-in Python functions, `sum`, which creates a sum from a list of numbers, and `len`, which will get the length of a list, tuple, or string:

```
with open(r'C:\Projects\Output\Averages.csv', 'wb') as csvfile:
    csvwriter = csv.writer(csvfile, delimiter=',')
    for busStopID in dataDictionary.keys():
        popList = dataDictionary[busStopID]
        averagePop = sum(popList)/len(popList)
        data = [busStopID, averagePop]
        csvwriter.writerow(data)
```

The average population value is retrieved from the dictionary using the Bus Stop ID key, and then assigned to the variable `averagePop`. The two data pieces, the `BusStopID` and the `averatePop` variable are then added to a list, which is supplied to a `CSVwriter` object, which knows how to accept the data and write it to a file located at the file path supplied to the built-in Python the `open()` function, used to create simple files.

The script is complete, although it is nice to add one more line at the end to give us visual confirmation that the script has run:

```
print "Data Analysis Complete"
```

This will create an output indicating that the script has run. Once it is done, go to the location of the output csv file and open it, using Excel or Notepad, and see the results of the analysis. Our first script is complete!

The final script

Here is how the script should look in the end:

```
# -*- coding: utf-8 -*-
# --------------------------------------------------------------------
----
# 8662_Chapter3Model1.py
# Created on: 2014-04-22 21:59:31.00000
#   (generated by ArcGIS/ModelBuilder)
# Description:
# --------------------------------------------------------------------
----

# Import arcpy module
import arcpy
import csv

# Local variables:
Bus_Stops = r"C:\Projects\PacktDB.gdb\SanFrancisco\Bus_Stops"
CensusBlocks2010 = r"C:\Projects\PacktDB.gdb\SanFrancisco\
CensusBlocks2010"
Inbound71 = r"C:\Projects\PacktDB.gdb\Chapter3Results\Inbound71"
Inbound71_400ft_buffer = r"C:\Projects\PacktDB.gdb\Chapter3Results\
Inbound71_400ft_buffer"
Intersect71Census = r"C:\Projects\PacktDB.gdb\Chapter3Results\
Intersect71Census"

# Process: Select
```

```
arcpy.Select_analysis(Bus_Stops,
                        Inbound71,
                        "NAME = '71 IB' AND BUS_SIGNAG = 'Ferry Plaza'")


# Process: Buffer
arcpy.Buffer_analysis(Inbound71,
                        Inbound71_400ft_buffer,
                        "400 Feet", "FULL", "ROUND", "NONE", "")


# Process: Intersect
arcpy.Intersect_analysis("{0} #;{1} #".format(Inbound71_400ft_
buffer,CensusBlocks2010),
                        Intersect71Census, "ALL", "", "INPUT")


dataDictionary = {}

with arcpy.da.SearchCursor(Intersect71Census, ["STOPID","POP10"]) as
cursor:
    for row in cursor:
        busStopID = row[0]
        pop10 = row[1]
        if busStopID not in dataDictionary.keys():
            dataDictionary[busStopID] = [pop10]
        else:
            dataDictionary[busStopID].append(pop10)


with open(r'C:\Projects\Output\Averages2.csv', 'wb') as csvfile:
    spamwriter = csv.writer(csvfile, delimiter=',')
    for busStopID in dataDictionary.keys():
        popList = dataDictionary[busStopID]
        averagePop = sum(popList)/len(popList)
        data = [busStopID, averagePop]
        spamwriter.writerow(data)


print "Data Analysis Complete"
```

Summary

In this chapter, we covered how to craft a model of an analysis and export it to a script. After discussing the script, we adjusted the script to include a results analysis and summation, which was outputted to a CSV file. In particular, we discussed how to use ModelBuilder to create an analysis and export it as a script, and how to adjust the script to be more Pythonic. We also briefly touched on the use of Search Cursors, which will be covered in greater detail in *Chapter 5, ArcPy Cursors – Search, Insert, and Update*. Also, we saw how built-in modules such as the CSV module can be used along with ArcPy to capture analysis output in formatted spreadsheets.

In the next chapter, we will discuss how to create more complex scripts and build functions to avoid repeating code. These functions will make it possible to write code once and use it forever. This reuse of code will demonstrate how Python goes beyond automation of analysis to become a new productivity toolset.

4
Complex ArcPy Scripts and Generalizing Functions

In this chapter, we will move from creating simple scripts based on autogenerated scripts from ModelBuilder to complex scripts that incorporate advanced Python and ArcPy concepts, such as functions. Functions can improve code and save time when writing scripts. They are also useful when creating modules or other reusable code, allowing for standard programming operations to be scripted and ready for future use.

In this chapter, will cover the following topics:

- Creating functions to avoid repeating code
- Creating helper functions to work with ArcPy limitations
- Generalizing functions to make them reusable

Python functions–Avoid repeating code

Programming languages share a concept that has aided programmers for decades: functions. The idea of a function, loosely speaking, is to create blocks of code that will perform an action on a piece of data, transforming it as required by the programmer and returning the transformed data back to the main body of code. We've already been introduced to some of Python's built-in functions in the last few chapters, the int function, for instance, will convert a string or a floating number into an integer; now it's time to write our own.

Functions are used because they solve many different needs within programming. Functions reduce the need to write repetitive code, which in turn reduces the time needed to create a script. They can be used to create ranges of numbers (the `range()` function), or to determine the maximum value of a list (the `max` function), or to create a SQL statement to select a set of rows from a feature class. They can even be copied and used in another script or included as part of a module that can be imported into scripts. Function reuse has the added bonus of making programming more useful and less of a chore. When a scripter starts writing functions, it is a major step towards making programming part of a GIS workflow.

Technical definition of functions

Functions, also called subroutines or procedures in other programming languages, are blocks of code that have been designed to either accept input data and transform it, or provide data to the main program when called without any input required. In theory, functions will only transform data that has been provided to the function as a parameter; it should not change any other part of the script that has not been included in the function. To make this possible, the concept of namespaces is invoked. As discussed in *Chapter 1*, *Introduction to Python for ArcGIS*, namespaces are used to isolate variables within a script; variables are either global, and available to be used in the main body of a script as well as in a function, or are local and only available within a function.

Namespaces make it possible to use a variable name within a function, and allow it to represent a value, while also using the same variable name in another part of the script. This becomes especially important when importing modules from other programmers; within that module and its functions, the variables that it contains might have a variable name that is the same as a variable name within the main script.

In a high-level programming language such as Python, there is built-in support for functions, including the ability to define function names and the data inputs (also known as parameters). Functions are created using the keyword `def` plus a function name, along with parentheses that may or may not contain parameters. Parameters can also be defined with default values, so parameters only need to be passed to the function when they differ from the default. The values that are returned from the function are also easily defined.

A first function

Let's create a function to get a feel for what is possible when writing functions. First, we need to invoke the function by providing the `def` keyword and providing a name along with the parentheses. The `firstFunction()` will return a string when called:

```
def firstFunction():
    'a simple function returning a string'
    return "My First Function"
```

```
>>>firstFunction()
```

The output is as follows:

```
'My First Function'
```

Notice that this function has a documentation string or doc string (a simple function returning a string) that describes what the function does; this string can be called later to find out what the function does, using the __doc__ internal function:

```
>>>print firstFunction.__doc__
```

The output is as follows:

```
'a simple function returning a string'
```

The function is defined and given a name, and then the parentheses are added followed by a colon. The following lines must then be indented (a good IDE will add the indention automatically). The function does not have any parameters, so the parentheses are empty. The function then uses the keyword `return` to return a value, in this case a string, from the function.

Next, the function is called by adding parentheses to the function name. When it is called, it will do what it has been instructed to do: return the string.

Functions with parameters

Now let's create a function that accepts parameters and transforms them as needed. This function will accept a number and multiply it by 3:

```
def secondFunction(number):
    'this function multiples numbers by 3'
    return number *3
```

```
>>> secondFunction(4)
```

The output is as follows:

```
12
```

The function has one flaw, however; there is no assurance that the value passed to the function is a number. We need to add a conditional to the function to make sure it does not throw an exception:

```
def secondFunction(number):
    'this function multiples numbers by 3'
    if type(number) == type(1) or type(number) == type(1.0):
        return number *3
>>> secondFunction(4.0)
```

The output is as follows:

```
12.0
```

```
>>>secondFunction(4)
```

The output is as follows:

```
12
```

```
>>>secondFunction("String")
```

```
>>>
```

The function now accepts a parameter, checks what type of data it is, and returns a multiple of the parameter whether it is an integer or a function. If it is a string or some other data type, as shown in the last example, no value is returned.

There is one more adjustment to the simple function that we should discuss: parameter defaults. By including default values in the definition of the function, we avoid having to provide parameters that rarely change. If, for instance, we wanted a different multiplier than 3 in the simple function, we would define it like this:

```
def thirdFunction(number, multiplier=3):
    'this function multiples numbers by 3'
    if type(number) == type(1) or type(number) == type(1.0):
        return number *multiplier
>>>thirdFunction(4)
```

The output is as follows:

```
12
>>>thirdFunction(4,5)
```

The output is as follows:

```
20
```

The function will work when only the number to be multiplied is supplied, as the multiplier has a default value of 3. However, if we need another multiplier, the value can be adjusted by adding another value when calling the function. Note that the second value doesn't have to be a number as there is no type checking on it. Also, the default value(s) in a function must follow the parameters with no defaults (or all parameters can have a default value and the parameters can be supplied to the function in order or by name).

These simple functions combine many of the concepts that we discussed in earlier chapters, including built-in functions such as `type`, `conditionals`, `parameters`, `parameter defaults`, and `function returns`. We can now move on to creating functions with ArcPy.

Using functions to replace repetitive code

One of the main uses of functions is to ensure that the same code does not have to be written over and over. Let's return to our example from the last chapter and make a function from the script to make it possible to perform the same analysis for any bus line in San Francisco.

The first portion of the script that we could convert into a function is the three ArcPy functions. Doing so will allow the script to be applicable to any of the stops in the Bus Stop feature class and have an adjustable buffer distance:

```
bufferDist = 400
buffDistUnit  = "Feet"
lineName = '71 IB'
busSignage = 'Ferry Plaza'
sqlStatement = "NAME = '{0}' AND BUS_SIGNAG = '{1}'"
def selectBufferIntersect(selectIn,selectOut,bufferOut,
                          intersectIn, intersectOut, sqlStatement,
                          bufferDist, buffDistUnit, lineName,
                          busSignage):
    'a function to perform a bus stop analysis'
```

```
arcpy.Select_analysis(selectIn, selectOut, sqlStatement.
                      format(lineName, busSignage))
arcpy.Buffer_analysis(selectOut, bufferOut,
                      "{0} {1}".format(bufferDist),
                      "FULL", "ROUND", "NONE", "")
arcpy.Intersect_analysis("{0} #;{1} #".format(bufferOut,
                         intersectIn), intersectOut, "ALL", "",
                         "INPUT")

return intersectOut
```

This function demonstrates how the analysis can be adjusted to accept the input and output feature class variables as parameters, along with some new variables.

The function adds a variable to replace the SQL statement and variables to adjust the bus stop, and also tweaks the buffer distance statement so that both the distance and the unit can be adjusted. The feature class name variables, defined earlier in the script, have all been replaced with local variable names; while the global variable names could have been retained, it reduces the portability of the function.

The next function will accept the result of the `selectBufferIntersect()` function and search it using the Search Cursor, passing the results into a dictionary. The dictionary will then be returned from the function for later use:

```
def createResultDic(resultFC):
    'search results of analysis and create results dictionary'
    dataDictionary = {}
    with arcpy.da.SearchCursor(resultFC, ["STOPID","POP10"])
                              as cursor:
        for row in cursor:
            busStopID = row[0]
            pop10 = row[1]
            if busStopID not in dataDictionary.keys():
                dataDictionary[busStopID] = [pop10]
            else:
                dataDictionary[busStopID].append(pop10)
    return dataDictionary
```

This function only requires one parameter: the feature class returned from the `searchBufferIntersect()` function. The results holding dictionary is first created, then populated by the search cursor, with the `busStopid` attribute used as a key, and the census block population attribute added to a list assigned to the key.

The dictionary, having been populated with sorted data, is returned from the function for use in the final function, createCSV(). This function accepts the dictionary and the name of the output CSV file as a string:

```
def createCSV(dictionary, csvname):
    'a function takes a dictionary and creates a CSV file'
    with open(csvname, 'wb') as csvfile:
        csvwriter = csv.writer(csvfile, delimiter=',')
        for busStopID in dictionary.keys():
            popList = dictionary[busStopID]
            averagePop = sum(popList)/len(popList)
            data = [busStopID, averagePop]
            csvwriter.writerow(data)
```

The final function creates the CSV using the csv module. The name of the file, a string, is now a customizable parameter (meaning the script name can be any valid file path and text file with the extension .csv). The csvfile parameter is passed to the CSV module's writer method and assigned to the variable csvwriter, and the dictionary is accessed and processed, and passed as a list to csvwriter to be written to the CSV file. The csv.writer() method processes each item in the list into the CSV format and saves the final result. Open the csv file with Excel or a text editor such as Notepad.

To run the functions, we will call them in the script following the function definitions:

```
analysisResult = selectBufferIntersect(Bus_Stops,Inbound71,
                                       Inbound71_400ft_buffer,
                                       CensusBlocks2010,
                                       Intersect71Census,
                                       bufferDist,
                                       lineName,
                                       busSignage )
dictionary = createResultDic(analysisResult)
createCSV(dictionary,r'C:\Projects\Output\Averages.csv')
```

Now, the script has been divided into three functions, which replace the code of the first modified script. The modified script looks like this:

```
# -*- coding: utf-8 -*-
# ---------------------------------------------------------------
----
# 8662_Chapter4Modified1.py
# Created on: 2014-04-22 21:59:31.00000
#    (generated by ArcGIS/ModelBuilder)
# Description:
# Adjusted by Silas Toms
```

```
# 2014 05 05
# --------------------------------------------------------------------
----

# Import arcpy module
import arcpy
import csv

# Local variables:
Bus_Stops = r"C:\Projects\PacktDB.gdb\SanFrancisco\Bus_Stops"
CensusBlocks2010 = r"C:\Projects\PacktDB.gdb\SanFrancisco\
CensusBlocks2010"
Inbound71 = r"C:\Projects\PacktDB.gdb\Chapter3Results\Inbound71"
Inbound71_400ft_buffer = r"C:\Projects\PacktDB.gdb\Chapter3Results\
Inbound71_400ft_buffer"
Intersect71Census = r"C:\Projects\PacktDB.gdb\Chapter3Results\
Intersect71Census"
bufferDist = 400
lineName = '71 IB'
busSignage = 'Ferry Plaza'
def selectBufferIntersect(selectIn,selectOut,bufferOut,intersectIn,
                          intersectOut, bufferDist,lineName, busSignage
):
    arcpy.Select_analysis(selectIn,
                          selectOut,
                          "NAME = '{0}' AND BUS_SIGNAG = '{1}'".
format(lineName, busSignage))
    arcpy.Buffer_analysis(selectOut,
                          bufferOut,
                          "{0} Feet".format(bufferDist),
                          "FULL", "ROUND", "NONE", "")
    arcpy.Intersect_analysis("{0} #;{1} #".format(bufferOut,intersectIn),
                          intersectOut, "ALL", "", "INPUT")
    return intersectOut

def createResultDic(resultFC):
    dataDictionary = {}

    with arcpy.da.SearchCursor(resultFC,
                          ["STOPID","POP10"]) as cursor:
        for row in cursor:
            busStopID = row[0]
            pop10 = row[1]
```

```
            if busStopID not in dataDictionary.keys():
                dataDictionary[busStopID] = [pop10]
            else:
                dataDictionary[busStopID].append(pop10)
    return dataDictionary

def createCSV(dictionary, csvname):
    with open(csvname, 'wb') as csvfile:
        csvwriter = csv.writer(csvfile, delimiter=',')
        for busStopID in dictionary.keys():
            popList = dictionary[busStopID]
            averagePop = sum(popList)/len(popList)
            data = [busStopID, averagePop]
            csvwriter.writerow(data)
analysisResult = selectBufferIntersect(Bus_Stops,Inbound71,
Inbound71_400ft_buffer,CensusBlocks2010,Intersect71Census,
bufferDist,lineName, busSignage )
dictionary = createResultDic(analysisResult)
createCSV(dictionary,r'C:\Projects\Output\Averages.csv')
print "Data Analysis Complete"
```

Further generalization of the functions, while we have created functions from the original script that can be used to extract more data about bus stops in San Francisco, our new functions are still very specific to the dataset and analysis for which they were created. This can be very useful for long and laborious analysis for which creating reusable functions is not necessary. The first use of functions is to get rid of the need to repeat code. The next goal is to then make that code reusable. Let's discuss some ways in which we can convert the functions from one-offs into reusable functions or even modules.

First, let's examine the first function:

```
def selectBufferIntersect(selectIn,selectOut,bufferOut,intersectIn,
                          intersectOut, bufferDist,lineName, busSignage
):
    arcpy.Select_analysis(selectIn,
                          selectOut,
                          "NAME = '{0}' AND BUS_SIGNAG = '{1}'".
format(lineName, busSignage))
    arcpy.Buffer_analysis(selectOut,
                          bufferOut,
                          "{0} Feet".format(bufferDist),
                          "FULL", "ROUND", "NONE", "")
    arcpy.Intersect_analysis("{0} #;{1} #".format(bufferOut,intersectIn),
                          intersectOut, "ALL", "", "INPUT")
    return intersectOut
```

This function appears to be pretty specific to the bus stop analysis. It's so specific, in fact, that while there are a few ways in which we can tweak it to make it more general (that is, useful in other scripts that might not have the same steps involved), we should not convert it into a separate function. When we create a separate function, we introduce too many variables into the script in an effort to simplify it, which is a counterproductive effort. Instead, let's focus on ways to generalize the ArcPy tools themselves.

The first step will be to split the three ArcPy tools and examine what can be adjusted with each of them. The Select tool should be adjusted to accept a string as the SQL select statement. The SQL statement can then be generated by another function or by parameters accepted at runtime (for example, passed to the script by a Script tool, which will be discussed in a later chapter).

For instance, if we wanted to make the script accept multiple bus stops for each run of the script (for example, the inbound and outbound stops for each line), we could create a function that would accept a list of the desired stops and a SQL template, and would return a SQL statement to plug into the Select tool. Here is an example of how it would look:

```
def formatSQLIN(dataList, sqlTemplate):
    'a function to generate a SQL statement'
    sql = sqlTemplate #"OBJECTID IN "
    step = "("
    for data in dataList:
        step += str(data)
    sql += step + ")"
    return sql

def formatSQL(dataList, sqlTemplate):
    'a function to generate a SQL statement'
    sql = ''
    for count, data in enumerate(dataList):
        if count != len(dataList)-1:
            sql += sqlTemplate.format(data) + ' OR '
        else:
            sql += sqlTemplate.format(data)
    return sql

>>> dataVals = [1,2,3,4]
>>> sqlOID = "OBJECTID = {0}"
>>> sql = formatSQL(dataVals, sqlOID)
>>> print sql
```

The output is as follows:

```
OBJECTID = 1 OR OBJECTID = 2 OR OBJECTID = 3 OR OBJECTID = 4
```

This new function, `formatSQL()`, is a very useful function. Let's review what it does by comparing the function to the results following it. The function is defined to accept two parameters: a list of values and a SQL template. The first local variable is the empty string `sql`, which will be added to using string addition. The function is designed to insert the values into the variable `sql`, creating a SQL statement by taking the SQL template and using string formatting to add them to the template, which in turn is added to the SQL statement string (note that `sql +=` is equivelent to `sql = sql +`). Also, an operator (OR) is used to make the SQL statement inclusive of all data rows that match the pattern. This function uses the built-in enumerate function to count the iterations of the list; once it has reached the last value in the list, the operator is not added to the SQL statement.

Note that we could also add one more parameter to the function to make it possible to use an AND operator instead of OR, while still keeping OR as the default:

```
def formatSQL2(dataList, sqlTemplate, operator=" OR "):
    'a function to generate a SQL statement'
    sql = ''
    for count, data in enumerate(dataList):
        if count != len(dataList)-1:
            sql += sqlTemplate.format(data) + operator
        else:
            sql += sqlTemplate.format(data)
    return sql
>>> sql = formatSQL2(dataVals, sqlOID," AND ")
>>> print sql
```

The output is as follows:

```
OBJECTID = 1 AND OBJECTID = 2 AND OBJECTID = 3 AND OBJECTID = 4
```

While it would make no sense to use an AND operator on ObjectIDs, there are other cases where it would make sense, hence leaving OR as the default while allowing for AND. Either way, this function can now be used to generate our bus stop SQL statement for multiple stops (ignoring, for now, the bus signage field):

```
>>> sqlTemplate = "NAME = '{0}'"
>>> lineNames = ['71 IB','71 OB']
>>> sql = formatSQL2(lineNames, sqlTemplate)
>>> print sql
```

The output is as follows:

```
NAME = '71 IB' OR NAME = '71 OB'
```

However, we can't ignore the Bus Signage field for the inbound line, as there are two starting points for the line, so we will need to adjust the function to accept multiple values:

```
def formatSQLMultiple(dataList, sqlTemplate, operator=" OR "):
    'a function to generate a SQL statement'
    sql = ''
    for count, data in enumerate(dataList):
        if count != len(dataList)-1:
            sql += sqlTemplate.format(*data) + operator
        else:
            sql += sqlTemplate.format(*data)
    return sql
```

```
>>> sqlTemplate = "(NAME = '{0}' AND BUS_SIGNAG = '{1}')"
>>> lineNames = [('71 IB', 'Ferry Plaza'),('71 OB','48th Avenue')]
>>> sql = formatSQLMultiple(lineNames, sqlTemplate)
>>> print sql
```

The output is as follows:

```
(NAME = '71 IB' AND BUS_SIGNAG = 'Ferry Plaza') OR (NAME = '71 OB' AND
BUS_SIGNAG = '48th Avenue')
```

The slight difference in this function, the asterisk before the data variable, allows the values inside the data variable to be correctly formatted into the SQL template by exploding the values within the tuple. Notice that the SQL template has been created to segregate each conditional by using parentheses. The function(s) are now ready for reuse, and the SQL statement is now ready for insertion into the Select tool:

```
sql = formatSQLMultiple(lineNames, sqlTemplate)
arcpy.Select_analysis(Bus_Stops, Inbound71, sql)
```

Next up is the Buffer tool. We have already taken steps towards making it generalized by adding a variable for the distance. In this case, we will only add one more variable to it, a unit variable that will make it possible to adjust the buffer unit from feet to meter or any other allowed unit. We will leave the other defaults alone.

Here is an adjusted version of the Buffer tool:

```
bufferDist = 400
bufferUnit = "Feet"
```

```
arcpy.Buffer_analysis(Inbound71,

                        Inbound71_400ft_buffer,

                        "{0} {1}".format(bufferDist, bufferUnit),

                        "FULL", "ROUND", "NONE", "")
```

Now, both the buffer distance and buffer unit are controlled by a variable defined in the previous script, and this will make it easily adjustable if it is decided that the distance was not sufficient and the variables might need to be adjusted.

The next step towards adjusting the ArcPy tools is to write a function, which will allow for any number of feature classes to be intersected together using the Intersect tool. This new function will be similar to the formatSQL functions as previous, as they will use string formatting and addition to allow for a list of feature classes to be processed into the correct string format for the Intersect tool to accept them. However, as this function will be built to be as general as possible, it must be designed to accept any number of feature classes to be intersected:

```
def formatIntersect(features):
    'a function to generate an intersect string'
    formatString = ''
    for count, feature in enumerate(features):
        if count != len(features)-1:
            formatString += feature + " #;"
        else:
            formatString += feature + " #"
    return formatString
>>> shpNames = ["example.shp","example2.shp"]
>>> iString = formatIntersect(shpNames)
>>> print iString
```

The output is as follows:

```
example.shp #;example2.shp #
```

Now that we have written the formatIntersect() function, all that needs to be created is a list of the feature classes to be passed to the function. The string returned by the function can then be passed to the Intersect tool:

```
intersected = [Inbound71_400ft_buffer, CensusBlocks2010]
iString = formatIntersect(intersected)
# Process: Intersect
arcpy.Intersect_analysis(iString,
                        Intersect71Census, "ALL", "", "INPUT")
```

Because we avoided creating a function that only fits this script or analysis, we now have two (or more) useful functions that can be applied in later analyses, and we know how to manipulate the ArcPy tools to accept the data that we want to supply to them.

More generalization of the functions

The other functions that we initially created to search the results, and generate the spreadsheet of results, can also be manipulated into being more generalized with a few tweaks.

If we want to generate more information about each census block within a distance to a bus stop (for example, if we had a census block dataset with income data as well as population data), we would pass to the function a list of attributes to be extracted from the final feature class. To make this possible, it would be necessary to adjust the createResultDic() function to accept this list of attributes:

```
def createResultDic(resultFC, key, values):
    dataDictionary = {}
    fields = [key]
    fields.extend(values)
    with arcpy.da.SearchCursor(resultFC, fields) as cursor:
        for row in cursor:
            busStopID = row[0]
            data = row[1:]
            if busStopID not in dataDictionary.keys():
                dataDictionary[busStopID] = [data]
            else:
                dataDictionary[busStopID].append(data)
    return dataDictionary
```

This new version of the createResultDic() function will generate a list of lists (that is, the values from each row are contained within a list and are added to a master list) for each bus stop, which can then be parsed later by knowing the position of each value in the list. This solution is useful when needing to sort data into a dictionary.

However, this is an unsatisfactory way to sort the results. What if the list of fields is not passed on to the dictionary and there is no way of knowing the order of the data in the lists? Instead, we want to be able to use the functionality of Python dictionaries to sort the data by field name. In this case, we will use nested dictionaries to create lists of results accessible by the type of data they contain (that is, population, income, or another field):

```
def createResultDic(resultFC, key, values):
    dataDic = {}
```

```
            fields = []
        if type(key) == type((1,2)) or type(key) == type([1,2]):
                fields.extend(key)
                length = len(key)
        else:
            fields = [key]
            length = 1
        fields.extend(values)
        with arcpy.da.SearchCursor(resultFC, fields) as cursor:
            for row in cursor:
                busStopID = row[:length]
                data = row[length:]
                if busStopID not in dataDictionary.keys():

                    dataDictionary[busStopID] = {}

                for counter,field in enumerate(values):
                    if field not in dataDictionary[busStopID].keys():
                        dataDictionary[busStopID][field] = [data[counter]]
                    else:
                        dataDictionary[busStopID][field].
    append(data[counter])
        return dataDictionary
>>> rFC = r'C:\Projects\PacktDB.gdb\Chapter3Results\Intersect71Census'
>>> key = 'STOPID'
>>> values = 'HOUSING10','POP10'
>>> dic = createResultDic(rFC, key, values)
>>> dic[1122023]
```

The output is as follows:

```
{'HOUSING10': [104, 62, 113, 81, 177, 0, 52, 113, 0, 104, 81, 177, 52],
'POP10': [140, 134, 241, 138, 329, 0, 118, 241, 0, 140, 138, 329, 118]}
```

In this example, the function is passed as parameters to a feature class, the STOPID, and the fields to be conglomerated. The fields variable is created to pass the required fields on to the Search Cursor. The cursor returns each row as a tuple; the first member of the tuple is busStopID, and the rest of the tuple is the data associated with that bus stop. The function then uses a condition to assess whether the bus stop has been previously analyzed; if not, it is added to the dictionary and assigned a second internal dictionary, which will be used to store the results associated with that stop. By using a dictionary, we can then sort through the results and assign them to the correct field to which they belong.

The previous example shows the results of requesting data for one particular bus stop (1122023). As there are two fields passed here, the data has been organized into two sets, and the field names are now keys for the internal dictionary. Because of this organization, we can now create averages for each field instead of just one.

Speaking of averages, we left the job of averaging the results of the search cursor analysis to the createCSV() function. This should also be avoided, as it reduces the usefulness of the createCSV() function by adding additional data manipulation duties that should be the responsibility of another function. Let's address this issue by adjusting the createCSV() function first:

```
def createCSV(data, csvname, mode ='ab'):
    with open(csvname, mode) as csvfile:
        csvwriter = csv.writer(csvfile, delimiter=',')
        csvwriter.writerow(data)
```

This is a stripped down version of the function, but it is infinitely more useful. By adjusting the function like this, we are limiting it to only doing two things: opening the CSV file and adding a row of data to it. Because we used the ab mode, if the CSV file exists, we will only be adding data to it instead of writing over it (if it doesn't exist, it will be created). This adding mode can be overridden by passing wb as the mode, which will generate a new script each time.

Now we can sort through the results of the analysis, average them, and pass them to our new createCSV script. To do this, we will iterate through the dictionary created by the createResultDic() function:

```
csvname = r'C:\Projects\Output\Averages.csv'
dataKey = 'STOPID'
fields = 'HOUSING10','POP10'
dictionary = createResultDic(Intersect71Census, dataKey, fields)

header = [dataKey]
for field in fields:
    header.append(field)

createCSV(header,csvname, 'wb' )

for counter, busStop in enumerate(dictionary.keys()):
    datakeys  = dictionary[busStop]
    averages = [busStop]
    for key in datakeys:
        data = datakeys[key]
        average = sum(data)/len(data)
        averages.append(average)
    createCSV(averages,csvname)
```

This last step shows how the CSV file is created: by iterating through the data contained in the dictionary and then averaging the values for each bus stop. Then, these averages are added to a list that contains the name of each bus stop (and the line it belongs to in this instance) and passed to the createCSV() function to be written into the CSV file.

Here is the final code. Note that I have converted many of the autogenerated comments into print statements to give some feedback on the state of the script:

```
# -*- coding: utf-8 -*-
# ---------------------------------------------------------------
# --------
# 8662_Chapter4Modified2.py
# Created on: 2014-04-22 21:59:31.00000
#   (generated by ArcGIS/ModelBuilder)
# Description:
# Adjusted by Silas Toms
# 2014 04 23
# ---------------------------------------------------------------
# --------


# Import arcpy module
import arcpy
import csv

Bus_Stops = r"C:\Projects\PacktDB.gdb\SanFrancisco\Bus_Stops"
CensusBlocks2010 = r"C:\Projects\PacktDB.gdb\SanFrancisco\
CensusBlocks2010"
Inbound71 = r"C:\Projects\PacktDB.gdb\Chapter4Results\Inbound71"
Inbound71_400ft_buffer = r"C:\Projects\PacktDB.gdb\Chapter4Results\
Inbound71_400ft_buffer"
Intersect71Census = r"C:\Projects\PacktDB.gdb\Chapter4Results\
Intersect71Census"
bufferDist = 400
bufferUnit = "Feet"
lineNames = [('71 IB', 'Ferry Plaza'),('71 OB','48th Avenue')]
sqlTemplate = "NAME = '{0}' AND BUS_SIGNAG = '{1}'"
intersected = [Inbound71_400ft_buffer, CensusBlocks2010]
dataKey = 'NAME','STOPID'
fields = 'HOUSING10','POP10'
csvname = r'C:\Projects\Output\Averages.csv'


def formatSQLMultiple(dataList, sqlTemplate, operator=" OR "):
    'a function to generate a SQL statement'
```

```
        sql = ''
        for count, data in enumerate(dataList):
            if count != len(dataList)-1:
                sql += sqlTemplate.format(*data) + operator
            else:
                sql += sqlTemplate.format(*data)
        return sql


def formatIntersect(features):
    'a function to generate an intersect string'
    formatString = ''
    for count, feature in enumerate(features):
        if count != len(features)-1:
            formatString += feature + " #;"
        else:
            formatString += feature + " #"
    return formatString



def createResultDic(resultFC, key, values):
    dataDictionary = {}
    fields = []
    if type(key) == type((1,2)) or type(key) == type([1,2]):
        fields.extend(key)
        length = len(key)
    else:
        fields = [key]
        length = 1
    fields.extend(values)
    with arcpy.da.SearchCursor(resultFC, fields) as cursor:
        for row in cursor:
            busStopID = row[:length]
            data = row[length:]
            if busStopID not in dataDictionary.keys():

                dataDictionary[busStopID] = {}

            for counter,field in enumerate(values):
                if field not in dataDictionary[busStopID].keys():
                    dataDictionary[busStopID][field] = [data[counter]]
                else:
```

```
                    dataDictionary[busStopID][field].
append(data[counter])

    return dataDictionary

def createCSV(data, csvname, mode ='ab'):
    with open(csvname, mode) as csvfile:
        csvwriter = csv.writer(csvfile, delimiter=',')
        csvwriter.writerow(data)



sql = formatSQLMultiple(lineNames, sqlTemplate)

print 'Process: Select'
arcpy.Select_analysis(Bus_Stops,
                    Inbound71,
                    sql)

print 'Process: Buffer'
arcpy.Buffer_analysis(Inbound71,
                    Inbound71_400ft_buffer,
                    "{0} {1}".format(bufferDist, bufferUnit),
                    "FULL", "ROUND", "NONE", "")

iString = formatIntersect(intersected)
print iString

print 'Process: Intersect'
arcpy.Intersect_analysis(iString,
                        Intersect71Census, "ALL", "", "INPUT")


print 'Process Results'
dictionary = createResultDic(Intersect71Census, dataKey, fields)


print 'Create CSV'
header = [dataKey]
for field in fields:
    header.append(field)
createCSV(header,csvname, 'wb' )


for counter, busStop in enumerate(dictionary.keys()):
```

```
    datakeys  = dictionary[busStop]
    averages = [busStop]

    for key in datakeys:
        data = datakeys[key]
        average = sum(data)/len(data)
        averages.append(average)
    createCSV(averages,csvname)

print "Data Analysis Complete"
```

Summary

In this chapter, we discussed how to take autogenerated code and make it generalized, while adding functions that can be reused in other scripts and will make the generation of the necessary code components, such as SQL statements, much easier. We also addressed when it is best not to go too far with the creation of functions to avoid making them too specific.

In the next chapter, we will investigate the powerful Data Access module and its Search Cursors, Update Cursors, and Insert Cursors.

5

ArcPy Cursors – Search, Insert, and Update

Now that we understand how to interact with ArcToolbox tools using ArcPy, and we have also covered using Python to create functions and import modules, we have a basic understanding of how to improve GIS workflows using Python. In this chapter we will cover data cursors and the Data Access module, introduced in 10.1. These data access cursors are a vast improvement on the cursors used in the arcgisscripting module (the precursor to ArcPy) and in earlier versions of ArcPy. Not only can the cursors search data, as we have seen, but they can update data using the Update Cursors and can add new rows of data using the Insert Cursor.

Data cursors are used to access data records contained within data tables, using a row by row iterative approach. The concept was borrowed from relational databases, where data cursors are used to extract data from tables returned from a SQL expression. Cursors are used to search for data, but also to update data or to add new data.

When we discuss creating data searches using ArcPy cursors, we are not just talking about attribute information. The new data access model cursors can interact directly with the shape field, and when combined with ArcPy Geometry objects, can perform geospatial functions and replace the need to pass data to ArcToolbox tools. Data access cursors represent the most useful innovation yet in the realm of Python automation for GIS.

In this chapter we will cover:

- Using Search Cursors to access attribute and spatial data
- Using Update Cursors to adjust values within rows
- Using insert cursors to add new data to a dataset
- Using cursors and the ArcPy Geometry object types to perform geospatial analyses in memory

The data access module

Introduced with the release of ArcGIS 10.1, the new data access module known as arcpy.da has made data interaction easier, and faster, than allowed by previous data cursors. By allowing for direct access to the shape field in a variety of forms (shape object, X values, Y values, centroid, area, length, and more), and a variety of formats (JavaScript Object Notation (JSON), Keyhole Markup Language (KML), Well Known Binary (WKB), Well-Known Text (WKT)), the data access module greatly increases the ability of a GIS analyst to extract and control shape field data.

The data access cursors accept a number of required and optional parameters. The required parameters are the path to the feature class as a string (or a variable representing the path) and the fields to be returned. If all fields are desired, using the asterisk notation and provide a list with an asterisk as a string as the field's parameter ([*]). If only a few fields are required, provide those fields as string fieldnames (for example ["NAME", "DATE"]).

The other parameters are optional but are very important, for both search and Update Cursors. A where clause in the form of a SQL expression can be provided next; this clause will limit the number of rows returned from the data set (as demonstrated by the SQL expression in the scripts in the last chapter). The SQL expressions used by the search and update cursors are not complete SQL expressions, as the SELECT or UPDATE commands are provided automatically by the choice of cursor. Only the where clause of the SQL expression is required for this parameter.

A spatial reference can be provided next in the ArcPy Spatial Reference format; this is not necessary if the data is in the correct format but can be used to transform data into another projection on the fly. There is no way to specify the spatial transformation used, however. The third optional parameter is a Boolean (or True/False) value that declares whether data should be returned in exploded points (that is, a list of the individual vertices) or in the original geometry format. The final optional parameter is another list that can be used to organize the data returned by the cursor; this list would include SQL keywords such as DISTINCT, ORBER BY, or GROUP BY. However, this final parameter is only available when working with a geodatabase.

Let's take a look at using `arcpy.da.SearchCursor` for shape field interactions. If we needed to produce a spreadsheet listing all bus stops along a particular route, and include the location of the data in an X/Y format, we could use the Add XY tool from the ArcToolbox. However, this has the effect of adding two new fields to our data, which is not always allowed, especially when the data is stored in enterprise geodatabases with fixed schemas. Instead, we'll use the SHAPE@XY token built into the data access module to easily extract the data and pass it to the `createCSV()` function from *Chapter 4, Complex ArcPy Scripts and Generalizing Functions,* along with the SQL expression limiting results to the stops of interest:

```
csvname = "C:\Projects\Output\StationLocations.csv"
headers = 'Bus Line Name','Bus Stop ID', 'X','Y'
createCSV(headers, csvname, 'wb')
sql = "(NAME = '71 IB' AND BUS_SIGNAG = 'Ferry Plaza') OR (NAME = '71 OB'
AND BUS_SIGNAG = '48th Avenue')"
with arcpy.da.SearchCursor(Bus_Stops,['NAME', 'STOPID', 'SHAPE@XY'], sql)
as cursor:
    for row in cursor:
        linename = row[0]
        stopid = row[1]
        locationX = row[2][0]
        locationY = row[2][1]
        locationY = row[2][1]
        data = linename, stopid, locationX, locationY
        createCSV(data, csvname)
```

Note that each row of data is returned as a tuple; this makes sense as the Search Cursor does not allow any data manipulation and tuples are immutable as soon as they are created. In contrast, data returned from Update Cursors is in list format, as lists can be updated. Both can be accessed using the indexing as shown previously.

Each row returned by the cursor is a tuple with three objects: the name of the bus stop, the bus stop ID, and finally another tuple containing the X/Y location of the stop. The objects in the tuple, contained in the variable `row`, are accessible using indexing: the bus stop name is at index 0, the ID is at index 1, and the location tuple is at index 2.

Within the location tuple, the X value is at index 0 and the Y value is at index 1; this makes it easy to access the data in the location tuple by passing a value as shown in the following:

```
locationX = row[2][0]
```

The ability to add lists and tuples and even dictionaries to another list or tuple or dictionary is a strong component of Python, making data access logical and data organization easy.

However, the spreadsheet returned from the previous code has a few issues: the location is returned in the native projection of the feature class (in this case, a State Plane projection), and there are rows of data that are repeated. It would be much more helpful if we could provide latitude and longitude values in the spreadsheet and the duplicate values were removed. Let's use the optional spatial reference parameter and a list to sort the data before we pass it to the createCSV() function:

```
spatialReference = arcpy.SpatialReference(4326)

sql = "(NAME = '71 IB' AND BUS_SIGNAG = 'Ferry Plaza') OR (NAME = '71 OB'
AND BUS_SIGNAG = '48th Avenue')"

dataList = []

with arcpy.da.SearchCursor(Bus_Stops, ['NAME','STOPID','SHAPE@XY'], sql,
spatialReference) as cursor:
    for row in cursor:
        linename = row[0]
        stopid = row[1]
        locationX = row[2][0]
        locationY = row[2][1]
        data = linename, stopid, locationX, locationY
        if data not in dataList:
            dataList.append(data)


csvname = "C:\Projects\Output\StationLocations.csv"
headers = 'Bus Line Name','Bus Stop ID', 'X','Y'
createCSV(headers, csvname, 'wb')
for data in dataList:
```

The spatial reference is created by passing a code representing the desired projection system. In this case the code for the WGS 1984 Latitude and Longitude geographic system is 4326 and is passed to the `arcpy.SpatialReference()` method to create a spatial reference object that can be passed to the Search Cursor. Also, the `if` conditional is used to filter the data, accepting only one list per stop into the list called dataList. This new version of the code will produce a CSV file with the desired data. This CSV could then be converted into a KML with the service provided by `www.convertcsv.com/csv-to-kml.htm`, or even better, using Python. Use string formatting and loops to insert the data into pre-built KML strings.

Attribute field interactions

Apart from the shape field interactions, another improvement offered by the data access module cursors is the ability to call the fields in a feature class by using a list, as discussed previously. Earlier data cursors required the use of a less efficient `get value` function call, or required the fields to be called as if they were methods available to the function. The new method allows for all fields to be called by passing an asterisk, a valuable method to access fields in feature classes that have not been inspected previously.

One of the more valuable improvements is the ability to access the Unique ID field without needing to know whether the data set is a feature class or a shapefile. Because shapefiles had a feature ID or FID, and feature classes had an object ID, it was harder to program a Script tool to access the unique ID field. Data access module cursors allow for the use of the `OID@` string to request the unique ID from either type of input. This makes the need to know the type of unique ID irrelevant.

As demonstrated previously, other attribute fields are requested by a string in a list. The field names must match the true name of the field; alias names cannot be passed to the cursor. The fields can be in the list in any order desired, and will be returned in the order requested. Only the required fields have to be included in the list.

Here is a demonstration of requesting field information:

```
sql = "OBJECTID = 1"
with arcpy.da.SearchCursor(Bus_Stops,
            ['STOPID','NAME', 'OID@'],
            sql) as cursor:
for row in cursor:
```

If the fields in the fields list were adjusted, the data in the resulting row would reflect the adjustment. Also, all of the members of the tuple returned by the cursor are accessible by zero-based indexing.

Update cursors

Update cursors are used to adjust data within existing rows of data. Updates become very important when calculating data or converting null values to a non-null value. Combined with specific SQL expressions, data can be targeted for updating with newly collected or calculated values.

Note that running code containing an Update Cursor will change, or update, the data on which it operates. It is a good idea to make a copy of the data to test out the code before running it on the original data.

All data access module Search Cursor parameters discussed previously are valid for Update Cursors. The main difference is that data rows returned by Update Cursors are returned as lists. Because lists are mutable, they can be adjusted using a list value assignment.

As an example, let's imagine that the bus line 71 will be renamed to the 75. Both inbound and outbound lines will be affected, so a SQL expression must be included to get all rows of data associated with the line. Once the data cursor is created, the rows returned must have the name adjusted, added back into the list, and the Update cursor's updateRow method must be invoked. Here is how this scenario would look in code:

```
sql = "NAME LIKE '71%'"
with arcpy.da.UpdateCursor(Bus_Stops, ['NAME'],sql),) as cursor:
    for row in cursor:
        lineName = row[0]
        newName = lineName.replace('71','75')
        row[0] = newName
```

The SQL expression will return all rows of data with a name starting with 71; this will include 71 IB and 71 OB. Note that the SQL expression must be enclosed in double quotes, as the attribute value needs to be in single quotes.

For each row of data, the name at position zero in the row returned is assigned to the variable lineName. This variable, a string, uses the replace() method to replace the characters 71 with the characters 75. This could also just be replacing 1 with 5 but I wanted to be explicit as to what is being replaced.

Once the new string has been generated, it is assigned to the variable `newName`. This variable is then added to the list returned by the cursor using list assignment; this will replace the data value that initially occupied the zero position in the list. Once the row value has been assigned, it is then passed to the cursor's `updateRow()` method. This method accepts the row and updates the value in the feature class for that particular row.

Updating the shape field

For each row, all values included in the list returned by the cursor are available for update, except the unique ID (while no exception will be thrown, the UID values will not be updated). Even the shape field can be adjusted, with a few caveats. The main caveat is that the updated shape field must be the same geometry type as the original row, a point can be replaced with a point, a line with a line, and a polygon with another polygon.

Adjusting a point location

If a bus stop was moved down the street from its current position, it would need to be updated using an Update Cursor. This operation will require a new location in an X/Y format, preferably in the same projection as the feature class to avoid any loss of location fidelity in a spatial transformation. There are two methods available to us for creating a new point location, depending on the method used to access the data. The first method is used when the location data is requested using the SHAPE@ tokens, and requires the use of an ArcPy Geometry type, in this case the Point type. The ArcPy Geometry types are discussed in detail in the next chapter.

```
sql = 'OBJECTID < 5'
with arcpy.da.UpdateCursor(Bus_Stops, [ 'OID@', 'SHAPE@'],sql) as cursor:
    for row in cursor:
        row[1] = arcpy.Point(5999783.78657, 2088532.563956)
```

By passing an X and Y value to the ArcPy Point Geometry, a Point shape object is created and passed to the cursor in the updated list returned by the cursor. Assigning a new location to the shape field in a tuple, then using the cursor's `updateRow()` method allows the shape field value to be adjusted to the new location. Because the first four bus stops are at the same location, they are all moved to the new location.

The second method applies to all other forms of shape field interactions, including the SHAPE@XY, SHAPE@JSON, SHAPE@KML, SHAPE@WKT, and SHAPE@WKB tokens. These are updated by passing the new location in the format requested back to the cursor and updating the list:

```
sql = 'OBJECTID < 5'
with arcpy.da.UpdateCursor(Bus_Stops, [ 'OID@', 'SHAPE@XY'],sql) as
cursor:
    for row in cursor:
        row[1] =(5999783.786500007, 2088532.5639999956)
```

Here is the same code using the SHAPE@JSON keyword and a JSON representation of the data:

```
sql = 'OBJECTID < 5'
with arcpy.da.UpdateCursor(Bus_Stops, [ 'OID@', 'SHAPE@JSON'],sql) as
cursor:
    for row in cursor:
        print row
        row[1] = u'{"x":5999783.7865000069, "y":2088532.5639999956,
                    "spatialReference":{"wkid":102643}}'
```

As long as the keyword, the data format, and the geometry type match, the location is updated to the new coordinates. The keyword method is very useful when updating points, however, the SHAPE@XY keyword does not work with lines or polygons as the location returned represents the centroid of the requested geometry.

Deleting a row using an Update Cursor

If we need to remove a row of data, the UpdateCursor has a deleteRow method that works to remove the row. Note that this will completely remove the data row, making it unrecoverable. This method does not require a parameter to be passed to it; instead, it will remove the current row:

```
sql = 'OBJECTID < 2'
Bus_Stops = r'C:\Projects\PacktDB.gdb\Bus_Stops'
with arcpy.da.UpdateCursor(Bus_Stops,
        ['OID@',
         'SHAPE@XY'],sql) as cursor:
    for row in cursor:
```

Using an Insert Cursor

Now that we have a grasp on how to update existing data, let's investigate using Insert Cursors to create new data and add it to a feature class. The methods involved are very similar to using other data access cursors, except that we do not need to create an iterable cursor to extract rows of data; instead, we will create a cursor that will have the special `insertRow` method that is capable of adding data to the feature class row by row.

The Insert Cursor can be called using the same `with..as` syntax but generally it is created as a variable in the flow of the script.

Note that only one cursor can be invoked at a time; an exception (a Python error) will be generated when creating two insert (or update) cursors without first removing the initial cursor using the Python del keyword to remove the cursor variable from memory. This is why the `with..as` syntax is preferred by many.

The data access module's Insert Cursor requires some of the same parameters as the other cursors. The feature class to be written to and the list of fields that will have data inserted (this includes the shape field) are required. The spatial reference will not be used as the new shape data must be in the same spatial reference as the feature class. No SQL expression is allowed for an Insert Cursor.

The data to be added to the feature class will be in the form of a tuple or a list, in the same order as the fields that are listed in the fields list parameter. Only fields of interest need to be included in the list of fields, meaning not every field needs a value in the list to be added. When adding a new row of data to a feature class, the unique ID will automatically be generated, making it unnecessary to explicitly include the unique ID (in the form of the `OID@` keyword) in the list of fields to be added.

Let's explore code that could be used to generate a new bus stop. We'll write to a test dataset called `TestBusStops`. We are only interested in the Name and Stop ID fields, so those fields along with the shape field (which is in a State Plane projection system) will be included in the data list to be added:

```
Bus_Stops = r'C:\Projects\PacktDB.gdb\TestBusStops'
insertCursor = arcpy.da.InsertCursor(Bus_Stops,
['SHAPE@', 'NAME','STOPID'])
coordinatePair = (6001672.5869999975, 2091447.0435000062)
newPoint = arcpy.Point(*coordinatePair)
dataList = [newPoint,'NewStop1',112121]
insertCursor.insertRow(dataList)
del insertCursor
```

If there is an iterable list of data to be inserted into the feature class, create the Insert Cursor variable before entering the iteration, and delete the Insert Cursor variable once the data has been iterated through, or use the with..as method to automatically delete the Insert Cursor variable when the iteration is complete:

```
Bus_Stops = r'C:\Projects\PacktDB.gdb\TestBusStops'
listOfLists = [[(6002672.58675, 2092447.04362),'NewStop2',112122],
               [(6003672.58675, 2093447.04362),'NewStop3',112123],
               [(6004672.58675, 2094447.04362),'NewStop4',112124]
               ]


with arcpy.da.InsertCursor(Bus_Stops,
        ['SHAPE@',
         'NAME',
         'STOPID']) as iCursor:
    for dataList in listOfLists:
        newPoint = arcpy.Point(*dataList[0])
        dataList[0] = newPoint
```

As a list, the `listOfLists` variable is iterable. Each list within it is considered as dataList in the iteration, and the first value in `dataList` (the coordinate pair) is passed to the `arcpy.Point()` function to create a `Point` object. The `arcpy.Point()` function requires two parameters, X and Y; these are extracted from the coordinate pair tuple using the asterisk, which 'explodes' the tuple and passes the values it contains to the function. The `Point` object is then added back into `dataList` using an index-based list assignment, which would not be available to us if the `dataList` variable was a tuple (we would instead have to create a new list and add in the `Point` object and the other data values).

Inserting a polyline geometry

To create and insert a polyline-type shape field from a series of points, it's best to use the SHAPE@ keyword. We will also further explore the ArcPy Geometry types, which will be discussed in the next chapter. When working with the SHAPE@ keyword, we have to work with data in ESRI's spatial binary formats, and the data must be written back to the field in the same format using the ArcPy Geometry types.

To create a polyline, there is one requirement, at least two valid points made of two coordinate pairs. When working with the SHAPE@ keyword, there is a methodology to converting the coordinate pairs into an ArcPy Point and then adding it to an ArcPy Array, which is then converted into an ArcPy Polyline to be written back to the shape field:

```
listOfPoints = [(6002672.58675, 2092447.04362),
                (6003672.58675, 2093447.04362),
                (6004672.58675, 2094447.04362)
                ]
line = 'New Bus Line'
lineID = 12345
busLine = r'C:\Projects\PacktDB.gdb\TestBusLine'
insertCursor = arcpy.da.InsertCursor(busLine, ['SHAPE@',
'LINE', 'LINEID'])
lineArray = arcpy.Array()
for pointsPair in listOfPoints:
    newPoint = arcpy.Point(*pointsPair)
    lineArray.add(newPoint)
newLine = arcpy.Polyline(lineArray)
insertData = newLine, line, lineID
```

The three coordinate pairs in tuples are iterated and converted into Point objects, which are in turn added to the Array object called lineArray. The Array object is then added to the Polyline object called newLine, which is then added to a tuple with the other data attributes and inserted into the feature class by the InsertCursor.

Inserting a polygon geometry

Polygons are also inserted, or updated, using cursors. The ArcPy Polygon Geometry type does not require the coordinate pairs to include the first point twice (that is, as the first point and as the last point). The polygon is closed automatically by the arcpy.Polygon() function:

```
listOfPoints = [(6002672.58675, 2092447.04362),
                (6003672.58675, 2093447.04362),
                (6004672.58675, 2093447.04362),
                (6004672.58675, 2091447.04362)
                ]
polyName = 'New Polygon'
```

```
polyID = 54321

blockPoly = r'C:\Projects\PacktDB.gdb\Chapter5Results\TestPolygon'

insertCursor = arcpy.da.InsertCursor(blockPoly,
['SHAPE@', 'BLOCK', 'BLOCKID'])

polyArray = arcpy.Array()

for pointsPair in listOfPoints:

    newPoint = arcpy.Point(*pointsPair)

    polyArray.add(newPoint)

newPoly = arcpy.Polygon(polyArray)

insertData = newPoly, polyName, polyID

insertCursor.insertRow(insertData)
```

Here is a visualization of the result of the insert operation:

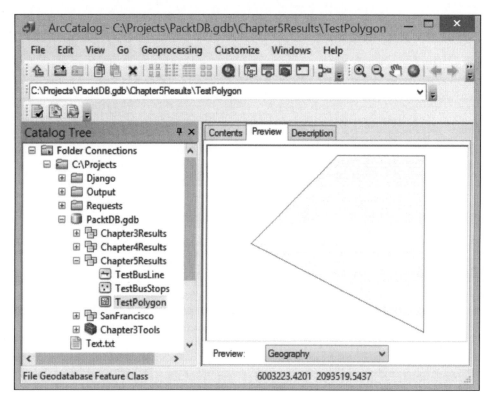

Summary

In this chapter we covered the basic uses of data access module cursors. Search, update and Insert Cursors were explored and demonstrated, and a special focus was placed on the use of these cursors for extracting shape data from the shape field. Cursor parameters were also introduced, including the spatial reference parameter and the SQL expression `where` clause parameter. In the next chapter, we will further explore the use of cursors, especially with the use of ArcPy Geometry types.

6

Working with ArcPy Geometry Objects

The essence of geospatial analysis is using geometric shapes – points, lines, and polygons – to model the geography of real world objects and their location-based relationships. The simple shapes and their geometric properties of location, length and area are processed using geospatial operations to generate analysis results. It is the combination of modeled geographic data and the associated attribute information that separate geospatial information systems from all other information systems.

Until ArcPy, processing the feature class geometry using the geospatial operations was depended on the pre-built tools within ArcToolbox. ArcPy has made it possible to directly access the geometric shapes which are stored as mathematical representations in the shape field of feature classes. Once accessed, this geometric data is loaded into ArcPy geometry objects to make the data available for analysis within an ArcPy script. Because of this advance, writing scripts that access geometry fields and use them to perform analysis has transformed ArcGIS geospatial analysis. In this chapter, we'll explore how to generate and use the ArcPy geometry objects to perform geospatial operations, and apply them to the bus stops analysis.

In this chapter, we will cover: `Point` and `Array` constructor objects and `PointGeometry`, `Polyline`, and `Polygon` geometry objects

- How to use the geometry objects to perform geospatial operations
- How to integrate the geometry objects into scripts
- How to perform common geospatial operations using the geometry objects
- How to replace the use of ArcToolbox tools in the script with geometry object methods

ArcPy geometry object classes

In designing geometry objects, the authors of ArcPy made it possible to perform geospatial operations in memory, reducing the need to use tools in the ArcToolbox for these operations. This will result in speed gains as there is no need to write the results of the calculations to disk at each step of the analysis. Instead, the results of the steps can be passed from function to function within the script. The final results of the analysis can be written to the hard drive as a feature class, or they can be written into a spreadsheet or passed to another program.

The geometry objects are written as Python classes- special blocks of code that contain internal functions. The internal functions are the methods and properties of the geometry objects; when called they allow the object to perform an operation (a method) or to reveal information about the geometry object (a property). Python classes are written with a main class that contains shared methods and properties, and with sub-classes that reference the main class but also have specific methods and properties that are not shared. Here, the main class is the ArcPy `Geometry` object, while the sub-classes are the `PointGeometry`, `Multipoint`, `Polyline` and `Polygon` objects.

The geometry objects are generated in three ways. The first requires using data cursors to read existing feature classes and passing a special keyword as a field name. The shape data returned by the cursor is a geometry object. The second method is to create new data by passing raw coordinates to a constructor object (either a `Point` or `Array` object), which is then passed to a geometry object. The third method is to read data from a feature class using the Copy Features tool from the ArcToolbox.

Each geometry object has methods that allow for read access and write access. The read access methods are important for accessing the coordinate points that constitute the points, lines and polygons. The write access methods are important when generating new data objects that can be analyzed or written to disk.

The `PointGeometry`, `Multipoint`, `Polyline`, and `Polygon` geometry objects are used for performing analysis upon their respective geometry types. The generic geometry object can accept any geometry type and an optional spatial reference to perform geospatial operations when there is no need to discern the geometry type.

Two other ArcPy classes will be used for performing geospatial operations in memory: the `Array` object and the `Point` object. They are constructor objects, as they are not sub-classed from the geometry class, but are instead used to construct the geometry objects. The `Point` object is used to create coordinate points from raw coordinates. The `Array` object is a list of coordinate points that can be passed to a `Polyline` or `Polygon` object, as a regular Python list of ArcPy `Point` objects cannot be used to generate those geometry objects.

ArcPy Point objects

Point objects are the building blocks used to generate geometry objects. Also, all of the geometry objects will return component coordinates as Point objects when using read access methods. Point objects allow for simple geometry access using its X, Y and Z properties, and a limited number of geospatial methods, such as contains, overlaps, within, touches, crosses, equals, and disjoint. Let's use IDLE to explore some of these methods with two Point geometry objects with the same coordinates:

```
>>> Point = arcpy.Point(4,5)
>>> point1  = arcpy.Point(4,5)
>>> Point.equals(point1)
True
>>> Point.contains(point1)
True
>>> Point. crosses(point1)
False
>>> Point.overlaps(point1)
False
>>> Point.disjoint(point1)
False
>>> Point.within(point1)
True
>>> point.X, Point.Y
(4.0, 5.0)
```

In these examples, we see some of the idiosyncrasies of the Point object. With two points that have the same coordinates, the results of the equals method and the disjoint method are as expected. The disjoint method will return True when the two objects do not share coordinates, while the opposite is true with the equals method. The contains method will work with the two Point objects and return True. The crosses method and overlaps method are somewhat surprising results, as the two Point objects do overlap in location and could be considered to cross; however, those methods do not return the expected result as they are not built to compare two points.

ArcPy Array objects

Before we progress up to `Polyline` and `Polygon` objects, we need to understand the ArcPy `Array` object. It is the bridge between the `Point` objects and those geometry objects that require multiple coordinate points. `Array` objects accept `Point` objects as parameters, and the `Array` object is in turn passed as a parameter to the geometry object to be created. Let's use Point objects with an Array object to understand better how they work together.

The `Array` object is similar to a Python list, with `extend`, `append`, and `replace` methods, and also has unique methods such as `add` and `clone`. The add method will be used to add `Point` objects individually:

```
>>> Point = arcpy.Point(4,5)
>>> point1  = arcpy.Point(7,9)
>>> Array = arcpy.Array()
>>> Array.add(point)
>>> Array.add(point1)
```

The `extend()` method would add a list of Point objects all at once:

```
>>> Point = arcpy.Point(4,5)
>>> point1 = arcpy.Point(7,9)
>>> pList = [Point,point1]
>>> Array = arcpy.Array()
>>> Array.extend(pList)
```

The `insert` method will put a `Point` object in the Array at a specific index, while the `replace` method is used to replace a `Point` object in an Array by passing an index and a new `Point` object:

```
>>> Point   = arcpy.Point(4,5)
>>> point1  = arcpy.Point(7,9)
>>> point2  = arcpy.Point(11,13)
>>> pList = [Point,point1]
>>> Array = arcpy.Array()
   >>> Array.extend(pList)
>>> Array.replace(1,point2)
>>> point3  = arcpy.Point(17,15)
>>> Array.insert(2,point3)
```

The `Array` object, when loaded with `Point` objects, can then be used to generate the other geometry objects.

ArcPy Polyline objects

The `Polyline` object is generated with an `Array` object that has at least two `Point` objects. As given in the following IDLE example, once an `Array` object has been generated and loaded with the `Point` objects, it can then be passed as a parameter to a `Polyline` object:

```
>>> Point   = arcpy.Point(4,5)
>>> point1  = arcpy.Point(7,9)
>>> pList = [Point,point1]
>>> Array = arcpy.Array()

>>> Array.extend(pList)
>>> pLine = arcpy.Polyline(Array)
```

Now that the Polyline object has been created, its methods can be accessed. This includes methods to reveal the constituent coordinate points within the polyline, and other relevant information:

```
>>> pLine.firstPoint
<Point (4.0, 5.0, #, #)>
>>> pLine.lastPoint
<Point (7.0, 9.0, #, #)>
pLine.getPart()
<Array [<Array [<Point (4.0, 5.0, #, #)>, <Point (7.0, 9.0, #, #)>]>]>
>>> pLine.trueCentroid
<Point (5.5, 7.0, #, #)>
>>> pLine.length
5.0
>>> pLine.pointCount
2
```

This example `Polyline` object has not been assigned a spatial reference system, so the length is unitless. When a geometry object does have a spatial reference system, the linear and areal units will be returned in the linear unit of the system.

The `Polyline` object is also our first geometry object with which we can invoke geometry class methods that perform geospatial operations, such as buffers, distance analyses, and clips:

```
>>> bufferOfLine = pLine.buffer(10)
>>> bufferOfLine.area
413.93744395
>>> bufferOfLine.contains(pLine)
True
>>> newPoint = arcpy.Point(25,19)
>>> pLine.distanceTo(newPoint)

20.591260281974
```

Another useful method of `Polyline` objects is the `positionAlongLine` method. It is used to return a `PointGeometry` object, discussed in the following, at a specific position along the line. This position along the line can either be a numeric distance from the first Point or as a percentage (expressed as a float from 0-1), when using the optional second parameter:

```
>>> nPoint = pLine.positionAlongLine(3)
>>> nPoint.firstPoint.X, nPoint.firstPoint.Y
(5.8, 7.4) >>> pPoint = pLine.positionAlongLine(.5,True)
         >>> pPoint.firstPoint.X,pPoint.firstPoint.Y

(5.5, 7.0)
```

There are a number of other methods available to `Polyline` objects. More information is available here: http://resources.arcgis.com/en/help/main/10.2/index.html#//018z00000008000000

ArcPy Polygon objects

To create a `Polygon` object, an `Array` object must be loaded with `Point` objects and then passed as a parameter to the `Polygon` object. Once the `Polygon` object has been generated, the methods available to it are very useful for performing geospatial operations. The geometry objects can also be saved to disk using the ArcToolbox `CopyFeatures` tool. This IDLE example demonstrates how to generate a `shapefile` by passing a `Polygon` object and a raw string filename to the tool:

```
>>> import arcpy
>>> point1 = arcpy.Point(12,16)
>>> point2 = arcpy.Point(14, 18)
>>> point3 = arcpy.Point(11, 20)
```

```
>>> Array = arcpy.Array()
>>> Points = [point1,point2,point3]
>>> Array.extend(points)
>>> Polygon = arcpy.Polygon(array)
>>> arcpy.CopyFeatures_management(polygon, r'C:\Projects\Polygon.shp')
<Result 'C:\\Projects\\Polygon.shp'>
```

Polygon object buffers

Polygon objects, like Polyline objects, have methods that make it easy to perform geospatial operations such as buffers. By passing a number to the buffer method as a parameter, a buffer will be generated in memory. The unit of the number is determined by the SpatialReference system. Internal buffers can be generated by supplying negative buffer numbers; the buffer generated being the area within the Polygon object at the specified distance from the Polygon perimeter. Clips, unions, symmetrical differences, and more operations are available as methods, as are within or contains operations; even projections can be performed using the Polygon object methods as long as it has a SpatialReference system object passed as a parameter. Following is a script that will create two shapefiles with two separate SpatialReference systems, each identified by a numeric code (2227 and 4326) from the EPSG coding system:

```
import arcpyPoint  = arcpy.Point(6004548.231,2099946.033)
point1  = arcpy.Point(6008673.935,2105522.068)
point2  = arcpy.Point(6003351.355,2100424.783)Array = arcpy.Array()
Array.add(point1)
Array.add(point)
array.add(point2)
Polygon = arcpy.Polygon(array, 2227)
buffPoly = Polygon.buffer(50)
features = [Polygon,buffPoly]
arcpy.CopyFeatures_management(features,
                          r'C:\Projects\Polygons.shp')
spatialRef = arcpy.SpatialReference(4326)
polygon4326 = Polygon.projectAs(spatialRef)
arcpy.CopyFeatures_management(polygon4326,
                          r'C:\Projects\polygon4326.shp')
```

Here is how the second shapefile looks in the **ArcCatalog Preview** window:

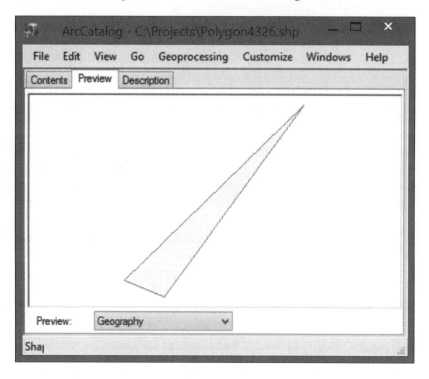

Other Polygon object methods

Unlike the clip tool in the ArcToolbox, which can clip a Polygon using another polygon, the clip method requires an extent object (another ArcPy class) and is limited to a rectangular envelope around the area to be clipped. To remove areas from a polygon, the difference method can work like the clip or erase tool in the ArcToolbox:

```
buffPoly = Polygon.buffer(500)
donutHole =buffPoly.difference(Polygon)
features = [Polygon,donutHole]
arcpy.CopyFeatures_management(features,
                      r"C:\Projects\Polygons2.shp")
```

Here is the donut hole-like result of the buffer and difference operation. The buffer with the donut hole surrounds the original `Polygon` object:

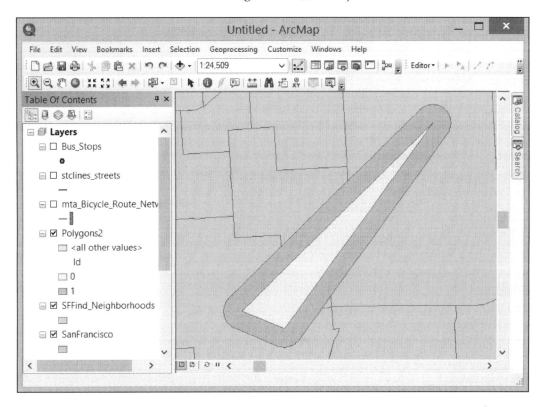

ArcPy geometry objects

The generic geometry object is quite useful for creating in memory a copy of the geometry of a feature class, without first needing to know which type of geometry the feature class contains. Like all of the ArcPy geometry objects, its read methods include the extraction of the data in many formats such as JSON, WKT, and WKB. The area (if it is a polygon), the centroid, the extent, and the constituent points of each geometry are also available, as demonstrated previously.

Here is an example of reading the geometry of a feature class into memory using the `CopyFeatures` tool:

```
import arcpy
cen2010 = r'C:\Projects\ArcPy.gdb\SanFrancisco\CensusBlocks2010'
blockPolys = arcpy.CopyFeatures_management(cen2010,
                                    arcpy.Geometry())
```

The variable `blockPolys` is a Python list containing all of the geometries loaded into it; in this case it is census blocks. The list can then be iterated to be analyzed.

ArcPy PointGeometry objects

The `PointGeometry` object is very useful for performing these same geospatial operations with points, which are not available with the `Point` objects. When a cursor is used to retrieve shape data from a feature class with a `PointGeometry` type, the shape data is returned as a `PointGeometry` object. While `Point` objects are required to construct all other geometry objects when a cursor is not used to retrieve data from a feature class, it's the `PointGeometry` object that is used to perform point geospatial operations.

Let's explore getting `PointGeometry` objects from a data access module `SearchCursor` and using the returned data rows to create buffered points. In our bus stop analysis, this will replace the need to use the ArcToolbox Buffer tool to create the 400 foot buffers around each stop. The script in the following uses a dictionary to collect the buffer objects and then searches the census blocks using another Search Cursor. To access the shape field using the `SearchCursor()` method, the `SHAPE@` token is passed as one of the fields. Then, the script will iterate through the bus stops and find all census blocks with which each stop intersects:

```
# Generate 400 foot buffers around each bus stop
import arcpy,csv
busStops = r"C:\Projects\PacktDB.gdb\SanFrancisco\Bus_Stops"
censusBlocks2010 = r"C:\Projects\PacktDB.gdb\SanFrancisco\
CensusBlocks2010"

sql = "NAME = '71 IB' AND BUS_SIGNAG = 'Ferry Plaza'"
dataDic = {}
with arcpy.da.SearchCursor(busStops, ['NAME','STOPID','SHAPE@'], sql) as
cursor:
    for row in cursor:
        linename = row[0]
```

```
    stopid = row[1]

    shape = row[2]

    dataDic[stopid] = shape.buffer(400), linename
```

Now that the data has been retrieved and the buffers have been generated using the buffer method of the `PointGeometry` objects, the buffers can be compared against the census block geometry using iteration and a Search Cursor. There will be two geospatial methods used in this analysis: `overlap` and `intersect`. The overlaps method is a boolean operation, returning a value of true or false when one geometry is compared against another. The `intersect` method is used to get the actual area of the intersect as well as identifying the population of each block. Using the intersect requires two parameters: a second geometry object, and an integer indicating which type of geometry to return (1 for point, 2 for line, 4 for polygon). We want the polygonal area of intersect returned to have an area of intersection available along with the population data:

```
# Intersect census blocks and bus stop buffers
processedDataDic = {} = {}
for stopid in dataDic.keys():
    values = dataDic[stopid]
    busStopBuffer = values[0]
    linename = values[1]
    blocksIntersected = []
    with arcpy.da.SearchCursor(censusBlocks2010,
    ['BLOCKID10','POP10','SHAPE@']) as cursor:
for row in cursor:
            block = row[2]
            population = row[1]
            blockid = row[0]
            if busStopBuffer.overlaps(block) ==True:
                interPoly = busStopBuffer.intersect(block,4)
                data = row[0],row[1],interPoly, block
                blocksIntersected.append(data)
    processedDataDic[stopid] = values, blocksIntersected
```

This portion of the script iterates through the blocks and intersects against the buffered bus stops. Now that we can identify the blocks that touch the buffer around each stop and the data of interest has been collected into the dictionary, it can be processed and the average population of all of the blocks touched by the buffer can be calculated:

```
# Create an average population for each bus stop
dataList = []
for stopid in processedDataDic.keys():
    allValues = processedDataDic[stopid]
    popValues = []
    blocksIntersected = allValues[1]
    for blocks in blocksIntersected:
        popValues.append(blocks[1])
    averagePop = sum(popValues)/len(popValues)
    busStopLine = allValues[0][1]
    busStopID = stopid
    finalData = busStopLine, busStopID, averagePop
    dataList.append(finalData)
```

Now that the data has been created and added to a list, it can be outputted to a spreadsheet using the `createCSV` module we created in *Chapter 4, Complex ArcPy Scripts and Generalizing Functions*:

```
# Generate a spreadsheet with the analysis results
def createCSV(data, csvname, mode ='ab'):
    with open(csvname, mode) as csvfile:
        csvwriter = csv.writer(csvfile, delimiter=',')
        csvwriter.writerow(data)


csvname = "C:\Projects\Output\StationPopulations.csv"
headers = 'Bus Line Name','Bus Stop ID', 'Average Population'
createCSV(headers, csvname, 'wb')
for data in dataList:
    createCSV(data, csvname)
```

The data has been processed and written to the spreadsheet. There is one more step that we can take with the data and that is to use the area of the intersection to create a proportional population value for each buffer. Let's redo the processing of the data to include the proportional areas:

```
dataList = []
for stopid in processedDataDic.keys():
    allValues = processedDataDic[stopid]
    popValues = []
    blocksIntersected = allValues[1]
    for blocks in blocksIntersected:
        pop = blocks[1]
        totalArea = blocks[-1].area
        interArea = blocks[-2].area
        finalPop = pop * (interArea/totalArea)
        popValues.append(finalPop)
    averagePop = round(sum(popValues)/len(popValues),2)
    busStopLine = allValues[0][1]
    busStopID = stopid
    finalData = busStopLine, busStopID, averagePop
    dataList.append(finalData)
```

Now the script is taking full advantage of the power of ArcPy geometry objects, and the script is running completely in memory which avoids producing any intermediate datasets.

Summary

In this chapter, we discussed in detail the use of ArcPy geometry objects. These varied objects have similar methods and are, in fact, sub-classed from the same Python class. They are useful for performing in-memory geospatial analyses, which avoids having to read and write data from the hard drive and also skips creating any intermediate data.

ArcPy geometry objects will become an important part of automating geospatial workflows. Combining them with Search Cursors makes ArcPy more useful than any earlier implementation of Python scripting tools for ArcGIS. Next, we will convert the raw script into a script tool that can be executed directly from the ArcToolbox or a personal toolbox in a geodatabase.

7
Creating a Script Tool

Now that the basics of creating and executing ArcPy scripts have been covered, we need to take the next step and create re-useable **Script tools**. Creating Script tools will allow for greater code reuse, and will make it easy to create custom tools for other GIS analysts and customers. With a Python script **backend** or code, and a familiar ArcGIS tool **frontend** or user interface, the particulars of the code are hidden from the user; it becomes just another tool, albeit a tool that can save days and weeks of work.

This chapter will cover the following topics:

- Adding parameters to scripts to accept input and produce output as required by the user
- Creating a custom tool frontend and a custom toolbox
- Setting the parameters of the tool frontend to allow it to pass arguments to the code backend

Adding dynamic parameters to a script

The scripts we have generated in previous chapters have all had **hard-coded** inputs. The input values were written in the script as strings or numbers and assigned to variables. While they can be updated manually to replace the input and output file paths and SQL statements, programmers should aim to create scripts that will not require editing each time they are used. Instead, scripts should be designed to be dynamic and accept file paths and other inputs as parameters or arguments, in much the same manner that the functions we have created accept parameters.

Python was designed with this in mind, and the sys module has a method called sys.argv that accepts inputs passed to the script when it is executed. While the designers of ArcPy and its predecessor arcgisscripting module initially took advantage of the sys.argv method, in time they designed an ArcPy method for accepting script parameters. As either method can be used when writing ArcPy scripts, and both are found in example scripts on the web, it is important to recognize the minute differences between the sys.argv method and arcpy. GetParameterAsText(). The major difference between the two methods is that sys. argv accepts the dynamic arguments as a list. Members of the list are accessed using list indexing and assigned to variables. Arcpy.GetParameterAsText() is a function that accepts an index number parameter. The index number passed reflects the order of the parameter within the tool's frontend; the first parameter is zero, the next is one, and so on.

 If the order of the parameters is adjusted in the tool frontend, this adjustment must be reflected in the code backend.

Displaying script messages using arcpy. AddMessage

It is important to receive feedback from scripts to assess the progress of the script as it performs an analysis. As basic as this would seem, Python scripts and programming languages in general do not, by default, provide any feedback except for errors and the termination of the script. This can be a bit discouraging to the novice programmer, as all built-in feedback is negative.

To alleviate this lack of feedback, the use of print statements allows the script to give reports on the progress of the analysis as it runs. However, when using a Script tool, print statements do not have any effect. They will not be displayed anywhere, and are ignored by the Python executable. To display messages in the script console when Script tools are executed, ArcPy has a arcpy.AddMessage() method.

Arcpy.AddMessage statements are added to scripts wherever feedback is required by the programmer. The feedback required is passed to the method as a parameter and displayed; whether it be a list, string, float or integer. Arcpy.AddMessage makes it easy to check on the results of analysis calculations, to ensure that the correct inputs are used and that the correct outputs are produced. As this feedback from the script can be a powerful debugging tool, use arcpy.AddMessage whenever there is a need for feedback from the Script tool.

Note that statements passed to `arcpy.AddMessage` will only display when the script is run as a Script tool.

Adding dynamic components to the script

To start making the script into a Script tool, we should first copy the script that we created in *Chapter 6, Working with ArcPy Geometry Objects* Chapter6_1.py, as Chapter7_1.py in a new folder called Chapter7. We can then start replacing the hard-coded variables with dynamic variables using arcpy.GetParameterAsText. There is another ArcPy method called GetParameter that accepts the inputs as an object, but for our purposes, GetParameterAsText is the method to use.

By adding arcpy.GetParameterAsText and arcpy.AddMessage to the script, we will have taken the first step towards creating a Script tool. Care must be taken to ensure that the variables created from the dynamic parameters are in the correct order, as reordering them can be time-consuming. Once the parameters are added to the script and the hard-coded portions of the script replaced with variables, the script is ready to become a Script tool.

First, move all of the variables that are hard-coded into the top of the script. Then, replace all of the assigned values with arcpy.GetParameterAsText, making them dynamic values. Each parameter is referred to using zero-based indexing; however, they are passed to a function individually instead of as a member of a list:

```
#Chapter 7.py
import arcpy, csv
busStops = arcpy.GetParameterAsText(0)
censusBlocks2010 = arcpy.GetParameterAsText(1)
censusBlockField = arcpy.GetParameterAsText(2)
csvname = arcpy.GetParameterAsText(3)
headers = arcpy.GetParameterAsText(4).split(',')
sql = arcpy.GetParameterAsText(5)
keyfields = arcpy.GetParameterAsText(6).split(';')
dataDic = {}

censusFields = ['BLOCKID10',censusBlockField, 'SHAPE@']
if "SHAPE@" not in keyfields:
```

```
    keyfields.append("SHAPE@")
```

```
arcpy.AddMessage(busStops)
```

```
arcpy.AddMessage(censusBlocks2010)
```

```
arcpy.AddMessage(censusBlockField)
```

```
arcpy.AddMessage(csvname)
```

```
arcpy.AddMessage(sql)
```

```
arcpy.AddMessage(keyfields)
```

As you can see from the variable `keyfields` and the variable headers, some further processing must be applied to certain variables, as not all of them are going to be used as strings. In this case, a list is created from the string passed to the variable `keyfields` by using the `string` functions split and splitting the string on every semi-colon, while the `headers` variable is created by splitting on the commas. To other variables, such as the `censusBlockField` variable and the variable keyfields, the `SHAPE@` keyword is added because it will be required each time the analysis is run. If a particular field is required for each run of the data, such as the `BLOCKID10` field, it can remain hard-coded in the script, or optionally could become its own selectable field parameter in the Script tool.

The variables will then be added to the remainder of the script in the correct places, making the script ready for the Script tool to become part of a custom Toolbox in a geodatabase or in ArcToolbox. However, we must first create the tool part of the Script tool for the values to be collected and passed to the script.

Creating a Script tool

Creating a script tool is a powerful combination of the power of ArcPy and the ease of use of the tools in ArcToolbox.

The first step is to create a custom toolbox to hold the script tool. To achieve this, do the following:

1. Open up **ArcCatalog** and right click in the **SanFrancisco.gdb** File Geodatabase.
2. Select **New** and then **Toolbox** from the menu.
3. Call the toolbox **Chapter8Tools**.
4. Right click on **Chapter8Tools**, select **Add**, and then select **Script**.

The following menu will appear allowing you to set up the script tool. Add a title with no spaces and a label, as well as a description. I prefer to run script tools in the foreground to see the messages it passes, but it is not necessary and can be annoying when needing to start a script and still work on other tasks. Click **Next** once the menu has been filled out.

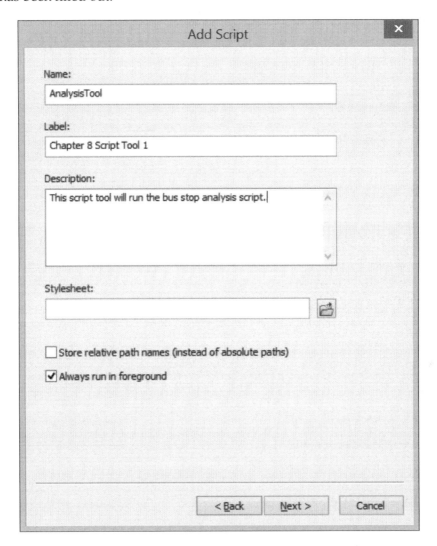

The next menu contains an entry field and a file dialog button, allowing the user to find the script to which the parameters collected will be passed. Use the file dialog to navigate to and select the script, and make sure that **Run Python script in process** is checked.

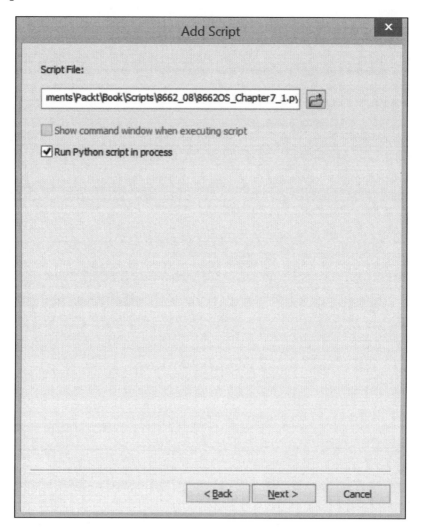

Now, push **Next** once the script has been identified.

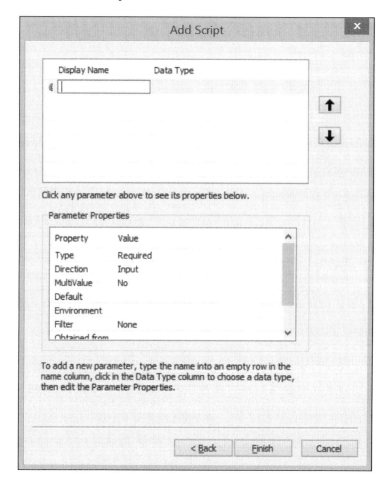

Labelling and defining parameters

The next dialog box is the most important one. It is where the parameters to be passed are labeled and their data types are defined. Care must be taken to choose the correct data type for each parameter as there are multiple data types that can be supplied for some of the parameters. Also, properties for each parameter will be defined; this information will characterize the data to be collected and help to make it possible for the data to be in the correct format as well as the correct data type.

Start by adding the display name for each parameter to be collected. The display name should explain the type of input that is required. For instance, the first parameter will be the bus stop's feature class, so the display name could be **Bus Stop Feature Class**.

Make sure to add the display names in the order that they will be passed to variables in the script.

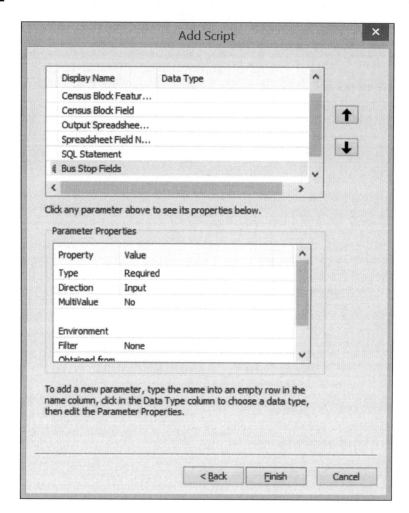

Adding data types

Next, add in the **Data Types** for each parameter. This is intricate because there will be a large list of data types to choose from, and often there are a few types that would work for many parameters. For instance, if a shapefile parameter is created, it would allow the user to select a shapefile as expected. However, it might be better to use the Feature Class data type, as then both shapefiles and feature classes could be used in the analysis.

Adding the Bus Stop feature class as a parameter

The first parameter is the **Bus Stop feature class**, and it should be a **Feature Class** data type. Click on the **Data Type Field** next to the display name and a drop-down list will appear. Once the data type is selected, check out the **parameter properties** below the list of parameters. For the Bus Stop feature class, the defaults will be acceptable, as the feature class is required, is not a multi-value, has no default or environment settings, and is not obtained from any other parameter.

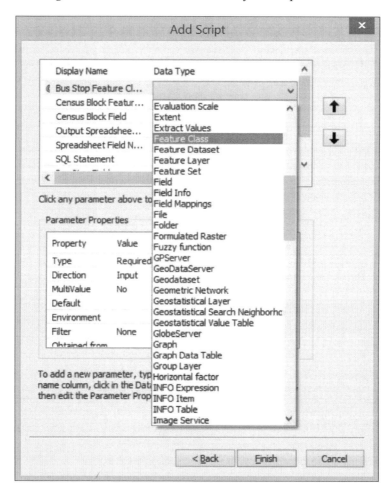

Some of the parameters will require another parameter to be selected first as they are derived values obtained from the first parameter. The Census Block Field parameter and the SQL statement parameter derive values from the Census Block feature class and Bus Stop feature class parameters, respectively.

Adding the Census Block feature class as a parameter

The Census Block feature class is similar to the Bus Stop feature class. It will be a Feature Class data type, allowing both shapefiles and feature classes to be selected, and there is no need to adjust the default parameter properties. Once the data type has been set, the **Census Block** parameter is ready for use.

Adding the Census Block field as a parameter

The **Census Block** field parameter has a new twist; it is obtained from the Census Block feature class parameter, and will only be populated once that first parameter has been created. To make this possible, the **Obtained from parameter** property will have to be set. Select **Field** as the data type, and then click on the blank area next to the **Obtained from parameter** property and select **Census_Block_Feature_Class**. This will create a list of the fields contained within the **Census Block feature class**.

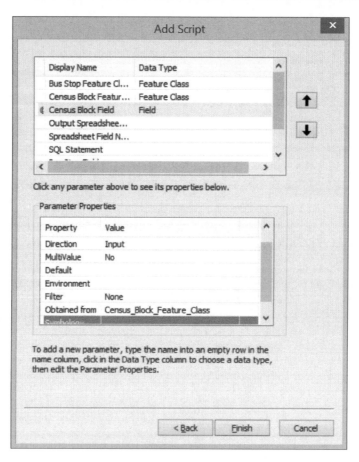

Adding the output spreadsheet as a parameter

As the spreadsheet that will be produced from the analysis run by the script tool is a **Comma Separated Value (CSV)** file, select **Text File** as the **Data Type**. Setting the **Default** parameter property to a file name can save time, and will make the required file extension easier to identify. Also, as the spreadsheet will be produced by the Script tool as an output, the **Direction** parameter property should be **Output**.

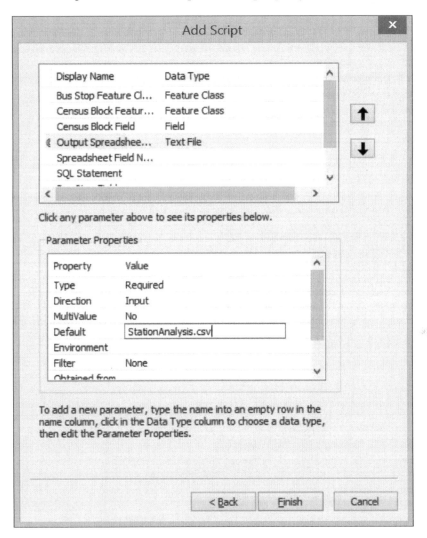

Adding the spreadsheet field names as a parameter

The field names chosen as headers for the output spreadsheet should be a **String** data type, with the field names separated by commas and no spaces. The script uses the string data type's `split` method to separate the field names. Passing a comma to the `split` method separates the parameter by **splitting** the input string on the commas to create a list of field names. The list of field names will be used as a header by the `csv` module when creating the spreadsheet.

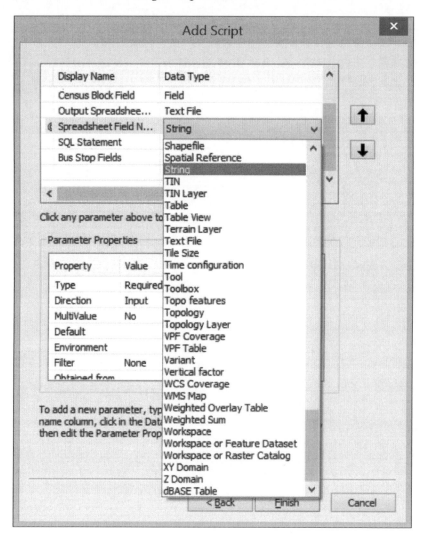

Adding the SQL Statement as a parameter

The **SQL Statement** parameter will require the helpful SQL Expression Builder menu and should therefore be a **SQL Expression** data type. The SQL Expression Builder will use a field obtained from the Bus Stop feature class. Set the `Obtained from parameter` property to the Bus Stop feature class by clicking on that property and selecting **Bus_Stop_Feature_Class** from the drop-down list.

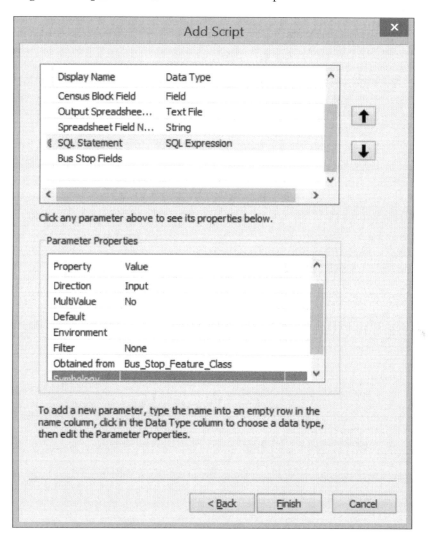

Adding the bus stop fields as a parameter

The final parameter is the bus stop fields parameter, which is a **Field** data type that will be obtained from the **Bus Stop feature class**. Change the **MultiValue** parameter property from **No** to **Yes** to allow the user to select multiple fields. Also remember to set the **Obtained from parameter** property to **Bus_Stop_Feature_Class** so that the fields are populated from the Bus Stop feature class parameter.

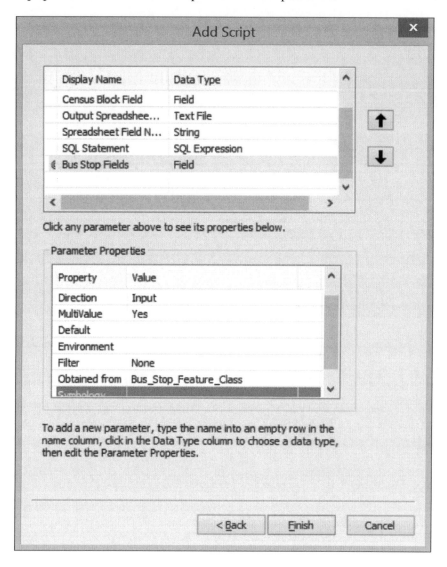

Now that all the parameters have been described and their properties have been set, the script tool is ready. Click on **Finish** to close the menu.

Inspecting the final script

Once all of the parameters have been collected, the variables are then used to replace the hard-coded field lists or other static script elements with the new dynamic parameters collected from the script tool. In this manner, the script has become a valuable tool that can be used for multiple data analyses, as the fields to be analyzed are now dynamic:

```python
import arcpy, csv
busStops = arcpy.GetParameterAsText(0)
censusBlocks2010 = arcpy.GetParameterAsText(1)
censusBlockField = arcpy.GetParameterAsText(2)
csvname = arcpy.GetParameterAsText(3)
headers = arcpy.GetParameterAsText(4).split(',')
sql = arcpy.GetParameterAsText(5)
keyfields = arcpy.GetParameterAsText(6).split(';')
dataDic = {}
censusFields = [ 'BLOCKID10',censusBlockField,'SHAPE@']
if "SHAPE@" not in keyfields:
    keyfields.append("SHAPE@")


arcpy.AddMessage(busStops)
arcpy.AddMessage(censusBlocks2010)
arcpy.AddMessage(censusBlockField)
arcpy.AddMessage(csvname)
arcpy.AddMessage(sql)
arcpy.AddMessage(keyfields)
x = 0
with arcpy.da.SearchCursor(busStops, keyfields, sql) as cursor:
    for row in cursor:
        stopid = x
        shape = row[-1]
        dataDic[stopid] = []
        dataDic[stopid].append(shape.buffer(400))
        dataDic[stopid].extend(row[:-1])
        x+=1


processedDataDic = {}
```

```
for stopid in dataDic.keys():
    values = dataDic[stopid]
    busStopBuffer = values[0]
    blocksIntersected = []
    with arcpy.da.SearchCursor(censusBlocks2010, censusFields) as cursor:
        for row in cursor:
            block = row[-1]
            population = row[1]
            blockid = row[0]

            if busStopBuffer.overlaps(block) ==True:
                interPoly = busStopBuffer.intersect(block,4)
                data = population,interPoly, block
                blocksIntersected.append(data)
    processedDataDic[stopid] = values, blocksIntersected


dataList = []
for stopid in processedDataDic.keys():
    allValues = processedDataDic[stopid]
    popValues = []
    blocksIntersected = allValues[-1]
    for blocks in blocksIntersected:
        pop = blocks[0]
        totalArea = blocks[-1].area
        interArea = blocks[-2].area
        finalPop = pop * (interArea/totalArea)
        popValues.append(finalPop)
    averagePop = round(sum(popValues)/len(popValues),2)
    busStopLine = allValues[0][1]
    busStopID = stopid
    finalData = busStopLine, busStopID, averagePop
    dataList.append(finalData)



def createCSV(data, csvname, mode ='ab'):
```

```
    with open(csvname, mode) as csvfile:

        csvwriter = csv.writer(csvfile, delimiter=',')

        csvwriter.writerow(data)


headers.insert(0,"ID")

createCSV(headers, csvname, 'wb')

for data in dataList:

    createCSV(data, csvname)
```

The variable x was added to keep track of the members of the dictionary dataDic, which in the script in *Chapter 6, Working with ArcPy Geometry Objects* had relied on the STOPID field. To eliminate this dependency, x was introduced.

Running the Script Tool

Now that the frontend has been designed to accept parameters from a user, and the backend script is ready to accept the parameters from the frontend, the tool is ready to be executed. Double click on the **Script Tool** in the toolbox to open the tool dialog box.

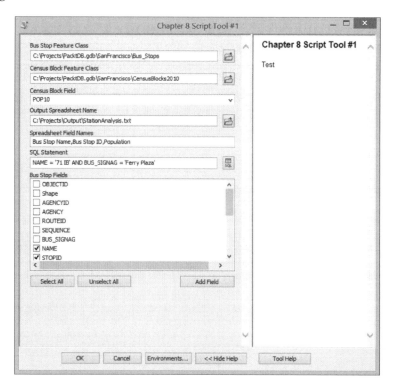

Select the parameters as with any ArcToolbox tool (for example using the file dialog to navigate a file tree to the **Bus Stop feature class**). Once the parameters have been set, click on **OK** to execute the script.

One optional adjustment would be to add an `arcpy.AddMessage` line where the average population is calculated. By doing this, the individual block population would be displayed and the script console would give feedback about the progress of the script.

Insert in the script just below the line where the variable `finalData` is defined:

```
arcpy.AddMessage(finalData)
```

The feedback provided by this line will make it obvious that the script is working, which is useful when the script executes a long analysis. When performing long analyses, it is good practice to provide feedback to the user so that they can see that the script is working as expected. Pass newline characters (\n) as parameters to `arcpy.AddMessage` when there is a large amount of data being passed to `arcpy.AddMessage`. This will break up the data into discrete chunks and make it easier to read.

Summary

In this chapter, we learned how to convert a script into a permanent and sharable script tool that can be used by an ArcGIS user with no programming experience. By creating a frontend using the familiar ArcGIS tool interface, and then passing parameters to custom built tools that employ ArcPy, GIS programmers can combine the ease of use of the ArcToolbox with the power of Python.

In the next chapter, we will explore how to use ArcPy to control the export of maps from map documents. By adjusting map elements such as titles and legends, we can create dynamic map outputs to reflect the nature of the data produced by map analysis. In *Chapter 9, More Arcpy.Mapping Techniques* we will add the output of maps to our script tool created in this chapter.

8
Introduction to ArcPy.Mapping

Creating maps is an art, one that can be learned through years of dedicated study of cartography. The visual display of information is both exciting and difficult, and can be a rewarding part of the daily workflow of geospatial professionals. Once the basics have been learned and mastered, cartographic output becomes a constant battle to produce more maps at a faster pace. ArcPy, once again, has a powerful solution: the `arcpy.mapping` module.

By allowing for the automatic manipulation of all map components, including the map window, the layers, the legend, and all text elements, `arcpy.mapping` makes creating, modifying, and outputting multiple maps fast and simple. Map book creation – another important skill for geospatial professionals, is also made easy using the module. In this chapter we will discuss some basic functionalities available through `arcpy.mapping` and use it to output a map book of bus stops and their surrounding census blocks.

This chapter will cover the following topics:

- Inspecting and updating Map Document (MXD) layer data sources
- Exporting MXDs to PDF or other image formats
- Adjusting map document elements

Using ArcPy with map documents

Recognizing the limitations of the previous arcgisscripting module, ESRI designed the ArcPy module to not only work with data but also included the arcpy.mapping module to allow direct interaction with map documents (MXDs) and the layers they contain. This new module opened up a multitude of map automation possibilities. A script might aid in identifying broken layer links, update the data source of these layers, and apply new color schemes to layers. Another script might use a map template and create a set of maps, one from each feature class in a feature dataset. A third script could create a map book from an MXD, moving from cell to cell in a grid layer to output the pages of the book, or even calculating the coordinates on the fly. Dynamically created maps, based on data from a fresh analysis, can be outputted at the same time the data is produced. Arcpy.mapping moves the ArcPy module from helpful to instrumental, in any geospatial workflow.

To investigate the utility of the arcpy.mapping module, we'll need the help of an MXD template. I've prepared a map package containing the data and MXD that we will use for the exercises in this chapter. It includes the data from our San Francisco bus stop's analysis, which we will continue and extend to include maps.

Inspecting and replacing layer sources

The first and most important arcpy.mapping module use is to identify and fix the broken links between layers in a map document and their data sources. Layer symbology and GIS data storage are separated, meaning that layer data sources are often moved. Arcpy.mapping offers a quick solution, though imperfect.

This solution depends on a number of methods included in the arcpy.mapping module. First, we will need to identify the broken links, and then we will fix them. To identify the broken links we will use the ListBrokenDataSources() method included in arcpy.mapping.

The ListBrokenDataSources() method requires an MXD path to be passed to the MapDocument() method of arcpy.mapping. Once the map document object has been created, it is passed to the ListBrokenDataSources() method, and a list will be generated containing layer objects, one for each layer with a broken link. The layer objects have a number of properties available to them. Using these properties, let's print out the name and data source of each layer using the name and data source properties of each object:

```
import arcpy
mxdPath = 'C:\Projects\MXDs\Chapter8\BrokenLinks.mxd'
mxdObject = arcpy.mapping.MapDocument(mxdPath)
```

```
brokenLinks = arcpy.mapping.ListBrokenDataSources(mxdObject)

for link in brokenLinks:

    print link.name, link.dataSource
```

Fixing the broken links

Now that we have identified the broken links, the next step is to fix them. In this case, it was revealed that the data sources should be in a folder called Data, but they are not contained within that folder. The script must then be stepped up to replace the data sources of each layer, so that they point at the actual location of the data source.

There are methods included in both layer objects and map document objects that can accomplish this next step. If all of the data sources for an MXD have been moved, it is better to use the MXD object and its methods to fix the sources. In the example MXD, the data sources have all been moved into a new folder called NewData, so we will employ the findAndReplaceWorkspacePaths() method to repair the links:

```
oldPath = r'C:\Projects\MXDs\Data'

newPath = r'C:\Projects'

mxdObject.findAndReplaceWorkspacePaths(oldPath,newPath)

mxdObject.save()
```

As long as the data sources are still in the same format (such that shapefiles are still shapefiles or feature classes are still feature classes), the findAndReplaceWorkspacePaths() method will work. If the data source types have been changed (such that, shapefiles are imported into a file geodatabase), the replaceWorkspaces() method will have to be used instead as it requires workspace type as a parameter:

```
oldPath = r'C:\Projects\MXDs\Data'

oldType = 'SHAPEFILE_WORKSPACE'

newPath = r'C:\Projects'

newType = 'FILEGDB_WORKSPACE'

mxdObject.replaceWorkspaces(oldPath,oldType,newPath,newType)

mxdObject.save()
```

Fixing the links of individual layers

If the individual layers do not share a data source, the layer objects will need to be adjusted using the findAndReplaceWorkspacePath() method available to layers. This method is similar to the method used previously, but it will only replace the data source of the layer object it is applied to instead of all of the layers. When combined with a dictionary, the layer data sources can be updated using the layer name property:

```
import arcpy
layerDic = {'Bus_Stops':[r'C:\Projects\OldDataPath', r'C:\Projects'],
            'stclines_streets': [r'C:\Projects\OtherPath',
            r'C:\Projects']}
mxdPath = r'C:\Projects\MXDs\Chapter8\BrokenLinks.mxd'
mxdObject = arcpy.mapping.MapDocument(mxdPath)
brokenLinks = arcpy.mapping.ListBrokenDataSources(mxdObject)
for layer in brokenLinks:
    oldPath, newPath = layerDic[layer.name]
    layer.findAndReplaceWorkspacePath(oldPath, newPath )
  mxdObject.save()
```

These solutions work well for individual map documents and layers. They can also be extended to folders full of MXDs by using the glob.glob() method of the built-in glob module (which helps to generate a list of files that match a certain file extension) and the os.path.join() method of the os module:

```
import arcpy, glob, os
oldPath = r'C:\Projects\MXDs\Data'
newPath = r'C:\Projects'
folderPath = r'C:\Projects\MXDs\Chapter8'
mxdPathList = glob.glob(os.path.join(folderPath, '*.mxd'))
for path in mxdPathList:
    mxdObject = arcpy.mapping.MapDocument(mxdPath)
    mxdObject.findAndReplaceWorkspacePaths(oldPath,newPath)
    mxdObject.save()
```

Exporting to PDF from an MXD

The next most important use of `arcpy.mapping` is to automatically export MXDs. The following code will highlight the export of PDFs, but note that the module also supports the export of JPEGs and other image formats. Using `arcpy.mapping` for this process is a joy, as the usual process of opening and exporting the MXDs involves a lot of waiting for ArcMap to start and the map to load, which can be a time sink:

```
import arcpy, glob, os
mxdFolder = r'C:\Projects\MXDs\Chapter8'
pdfFolder = r'C:\Projects\PDFs\Chapter8'
mxdPathList = glob.glob(os.path.join(mxdFolder, '*.mxd'))
for mxdPath in mxdPathList:
    mxdObject = arcpy.mapping.MapDocument(mxdPath)
    arcpy.mapping.ExportToPDF(mxdObject,
                            os.path.join(pdfFolder,
                            basepath(
            mxdPath.replace('mxd','pdf')
            ))))
```

 Note that the output folder must exist for this code to run correctly. While there are `os` module methods to check whether a path exists (`os.path.exists`) and to create a folder (`os.mkdir`), that is not included in this code snippet and the `arcpy.mapping.ExportToPDF()` method will throw an exception if the input or output paths do not exist.

This example code is very useful and can be converted into a function that would accept the folder path as a parameter. The function could then be added to a script tool, as discussed in the last chapter.

Adjusting map document elements

`Arcpy.mapping` includes important methods that will facilitate the automation of map document manipulation. These include the ability to add new layers or turn layers on and off within MXDs, the ability to adjust the scale of the data frame or move a data frame to focus on a specific region, and the ability to adjust text components of the map (such as titles or subtitles). These methods will be addressed as we continue our bus stop analysis.

Open up the MXD called MapAdjust.mxd. This represents our base map document, with layers and elements that we will adjust to our needs. It contains layers that we have generated from our analysis, and the base layers that fill out the map. There are also a number of text elements that will be automatically replaced by the script to fit the specific needs of each map. However, it does not do a good job of representing the results of the analysis as the census blocks that intersect the bus stop buffers overlap, making it hard to interpret the cartography.

The script will replace the data source of the census block layer and the bus stop layer to make it possible to only produce one map for each bus stop, and the census blocks that are intersected with each buffer surrounding the stops.

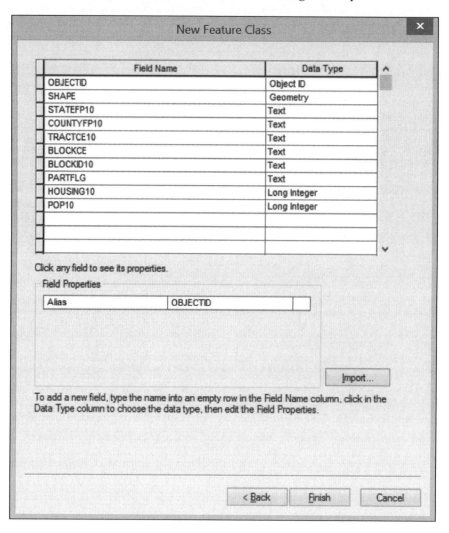

To make this possible, we will have to create two empty feature classes: one, with all of the attributes of the census blocks, and the other, with the attributes of the bus stops. This will allow the data source to be replaced with the data produced by the analysis.

Open up the SanFrancisco.gdb File Geodatabase and right click on the Chapter8Results feature dataset. Select **New** from the drop-down menu and then select **Feature Class. Name** the first feature class SelectedCensusBlocks and make it a polygon. Select the **defaults keyword** on the next menu, and then on the following menu, push the **import** button. Select the **CensusBlocks** feature class from the SanFrancisco feature dataset; this will load the fields into the new feature class. Do the same thing for a second feature class called SelectedBusStops, but make sure that it is a point geometry type and import the schema from the BusStops feature class. Repeat the same process for a third feature class called SelectedStopBuffers, but make sure that it is a point geometry type and import the schema from the Buffers feature class.

Once the feature classes have been created, it is now possible to use them to load the results of the analysis. We will be redoing the analysis in memory and writing out the results to the newly created feature classes, so that the entire census block will be captured, instead of only the portion that intersects with the buffer, as it will better illustrate the results of the analysis.

The initial state of the MapAdjust.mxd map document features a number of feature classes with which we are now familiar: the downloaded feature class Bus_Stops, the generated feature class Buffers, the intersected and clipped Census Blocks, and four feature classes used for cartographic purposes, namely the **Streets feature** class, the **Parks feature** class, a **Neighborhoods feature** class, and an outline of **San Francisco**. There are two data frames, one with the default name **Layers** and another called **Inset**, that are used to create the small inset that will show the position of the Layers data frame as it moves around San Francisco. The small rectangle that depicts the extent of the Layers data frame is an Extent frame created in the properties of the Inset data frame.

Here is an exported view of the initial state of the map document:

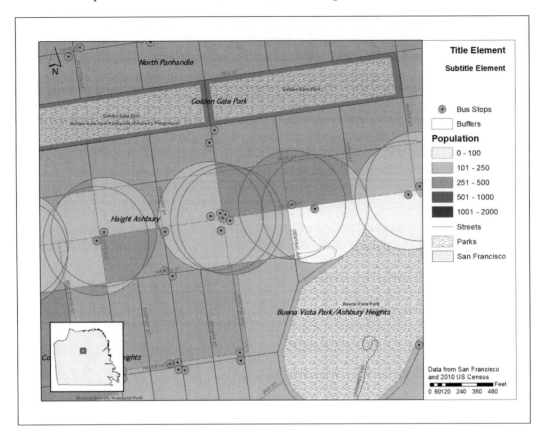

The idea here, is to use the initial results of our analysis to generate the symbology of the population layer as well as the bus stop layer and the buffer layer. Once they have been set and saved, they can be used as a basis for the individual map pages that we will be producing from this basic map document.

 Note the text elements that make up the title and subtitle, as well as the legend and attribution text at the bottom of the right pane. These elements are available for adjustment along with the layers and data sources that make up the map document by using the `arcpy.mapping.ListElements()` method.

Automated map document adjustment

Now that we understand the initial configuration of the map document, we will introduce a script that will automate the adjustment. This script will include a number of concepts that we have covered in this chapter and earlier chapters, and will also introduce some new methods for map document adjustments that we will detail in the following:

```
import arcpy, os
dirpath = os.path.dirname
basepath = os.path.basename
Bus_Stops = r"C:\Projects\SanFrancisco.gdb\Bus_Stops"
selectedBusStop = r'C:\Projects\SanFrancisco.gdb\Chapter8Results\
SelectedBusStop'
selectedStopBuffer = r'C:\Projects\SanFrancisco.gdb\Chapter8Results\
SelectedStopBuffer'
CensusBlocks2010 = r"C:\Projects\SanFrancisco.gdb\CensusBlocks2010"
selectedBlock = r'C:\Projects\SanFrancisco.gdb\Chapter8Results\
SelectedCensusData'
pdfFolder = r'C:\Projects\PDFs\Chapter8\Map_{0}'
bufferDist = 400
sql = "(NAME = '71 IB' AND BUS_SIGNAG = 'Ferry Plaza')"
mxdObject = arcpy.mapping.MapDocument("CURRENT")
dataFrame = arcpy.mapping.ListDataFrames(mxdObject, "Layers")[0]
elements = arcpy.mapping.ListLayoutElements(mxdObject)
for el in elements:
    if el.type =="TEXT_ELEMENT":
        if el.text == 'Title Element':
            titleText = el
        elif el.text == 'Subtitle Element':
            subTitleText = el
arcpy.MakeFeatureLayer_management(CensusBlocks2010, 'blocks_lyr')
layersList = arcpy.mapping.ListLayers(mxdObject,"",dataFrame)
layerStops = layersList[0]
layerCensus = layersList[1]
layerBuffer = layersList[2]
layerBlocks = layersList[3]
if layerBlocks.dataSource != selectedBlock:
```

```
        layerBlocks.replaceDataSource(dirpath(dirpath(layerBlocks.
dataSource)),
                                      'FILEGDB_WORKSPACE',basepath
                                      (selectedBlock))
if layerStops.dataSource != selectedBusStop:
    layerStops.replaceDataSource(dirpath(dirpath(layerStops.dataSource)),
                                      'FILEGDB_WORKSPACE',basepath
                                      (selectedBusStop))
if layerBuffer.dataSource != selectedStopBuffer:
    layerBuffer.replaceDataSource(dirpath(dirpath(layerBuffer.
                                      dataSource)),
                                      'FILEGDB_WORKSPACE',basepath
                                      (selectedStopBuffer))
layerStops.visible = True
layerBuffer.visible = True
layerCensus.visible = False
with arcpy.da.SearchCursor(Bus_Stops,['SHAPE@','STOPID','NAME',
                                      'BUS_SIGNAG' ,'OID@','SHAPE@
                                      XY'],sql) as cursor:
    for row in cursor:
        stopPointGeometry = row[0]
        stopBuffer = stopPointGeometry.buffer(bufferDist)
        with arcpy.da.UpdateCursor(layerBlocks,['OID@']) as dcursor:
            for drow in dcursor:
                dcursor.deleteRow()
        arcpy.SelectLayerByLocation_management('blocks_lyr', 'intersect',
                                        stopBuffer, "",
                                        "NEW_SELECTION")
        with arcpy.da.SearchCursor('blocks_lyr',['SHAPE@','POP10','OID@'])
        as bcursor:
            inCursor = arcpy.da.InsertCursor(selectedBlock,['SHAPE@',
                                        'POP10'])
            for drow in bcursor:
                data = drow[0],drow[1]
                inCursor.insertRow(data)
        del inCursor
        with arcpy.da.UpdateCursor(selectedBusStop,['OID@']) as dcursor:
            for drow in dcursor:
                dcursor.deleteRow()
```

```
        inBusStopCursor = arcpy.da.InsertCursor(selectedBusStop,
                                        ['SHAPE@'])

        data = [row[0]]

        inBusStopCursor.insertRow(data)

        del inBusStopCursor

        with arcpy.da.UpdateCursor(selectedStopBuffer, ['OID@']) as
dcursor:
                for drow in dcursor:
                        dcursor.deleteRow()

        inBufferCursor = arcpy.da.InsertCursor(selectedStopBuffer,
                                        ['SHAPE@'])

        data = [stopBuffer]

        inBufferCursor.insertRow(data)

        del inBufferCursor

        layerStops.name = "Stop #{0}".format(row[1])

        arcpy.RefreshActiveView()

        dataFrame.extent = arcpy.Extent(row[-1][0]-1200,row[-1][1]-1200,
                                        row[-1][0]+1200,row[-1][1]-1200)

        subTitleText.text = "Route {0}".format(row[2])

        titleText.text = "Bus Stop {0}".format(row[1])

        outPath  = pdfFolder.format( str(row[1])+ "_" + str(row[-2])) +
'.pdf'

        print outPath

        arcpy.mapping.ExportToPDF(mxdObject,outPath)

        titleText.text = 'Title Element'

        subTitleText.text = 'Subtitle Element'

        arcpy.RefreshActiveView()
```

Wow! That's a lot of code. Let's review it section by section to address what each part of the script is doing.

This code will be run in the Python Window of the MXD, so make sure to open the MXD. Once it is, open the **Python** Window and right click in it, and then select **Load** from the right-click menu. Using the file navigation browser, find the script called Chapter8_6_AdjustmapCURRENT.py and select it by clicking on it. Push **OK** and it will load in the Python Window. Pushing **Enter** will execute the script, or use the scroll bar to peruse the loaded lines.

The variables

Within the script, a number of variables are first created to hold the `string` file paths, the `integer` buffer distance, and the `sql` statement used to identify the bus line of interest:

```
import arcpy, os
Bus_Stops = r"C:\Projects\SanFrancisco.gdb\Bus_Stops"
selectedBusStop = r'C:\Projects\SanFrancisco.gdb\Chapter8Results\
                SelectedBusStop'
selectedStopBuffer = r'C:\Projects\SanFrancisco.gdb\Chapter8Results\
                SelectedStopBuffer'
CensusBlocks2010 = r"C:\Projects\SanFrancisco.gdb\CensusBlocks2010"
selectedBlock = r'C:\Projects\SanFrancisco.gdb\Chapter8Results\
                SelectedCensusData'
pdfFolder = r'C:\Projects\PDFs\Chapter8\Map_{0}'
bufferDist = 400
sql = "(NAME = '71 IB' AND BUS_SIGNAG = 'Ferry Plaza')"
```

These will be used later to allow us to search the layers and perform analysis on them.

The map document object and the text elements

Because this code will be executed in an open map document, we don't have to pass an MXD file path to the `arcpy.mapping.MapDocument()` method. Instead, we will use the keyword CURRENT to indicate that we are referencing the open map document:

```
mxdObject = arcpy.mapping.MapDocument("CURRENT")
dataFrame = arcpy.mapping.ListDataFrames(mxdObject, "Layers")[0]
elements = arcpy.mapping.ListLayoutElements(mxdObject)
for el in elements:
    if el.type =="TEXT_ELEMENT":
        if el.text == 'Title Element':
            titleText = el
        elif el.text == 'Subtitle Element':
            subTitleText = el
```

Once the map document object has been created, the Layers data frame is selected from a list of data frames using the `ListDataFrames()` method and passed to the variable called dataFrame.

Next, the layout elements are passed as a list to the elements variable using the `ListLayoutElements()` method. The layout elements include the various elements of the map document layout view: the legend, the neat lines, the north arrow, the scale bar, and the text elements used as titles and descriptions. Unfortunately, there is no nice order to the list returned, as their position throughout the layout is undetermined. Access to the text elements, which we would like to assign to a variable for later use, must be identified using two properties of the element objects: the type and the text. We want to adjust the title and subtitle elements, so a `for` loop is used to search through the list of elements and the properties are used to find the elements of interest.

The layer objects

The Make Feature Layer tool, part of the Data Management toolset, is used to copy data from disk into memory as a layer. ArcGIS requires the generation of layers to perform selections and operations on data, instead of operating on the feature classes directly. By using layers to perform these operations, the source feature classes are protected.

The Make Feature Layer tool is accessed using ArcPy's `MakeFeatureLayer_management()` method. When using this tool in the Python Window, the result is added to the map document as a layer that will be visible in the Table of Contents. When the tool is not used in the Python Window in ArcMap, the resulting layer is only generated in memory and is not added to the map document.

In the portion of the following code, a layer called `blocks_lyr` is generated in memory by passing the file path of the census blocks feature class. The layer objects contained within the initial MXD are then accessed using the `ListLayers()` method of the `arcpy.mapping()` module. They are returned in the order that they are listed in the Table of Contents of the map document and are assigned to variables using list indexing, including the newly created `blocks_lyr`:

```
arcpy.MakeFeatureLayer_management(CensusBlocks2010, 'blocks_lyr')
layersList = arcpy.mapping.ListLayers(mxdObject,"",dataFrame)
layerStops = layersList[0]
layerCensus = layersList[1]
layerBuffer = layersList[2]
layerBlocks = layersList[3]
```

Replacing the data sources

Now that we have assigned the layer objects to variables, we will check whether their data sources are the correct feature classes that we use for map production. Using the dataSource property of each layer object, they are compared to the file path variables that we want to use as data sources:

```
if layerBlocks.dataSource != selectedBlock:
    layerBlocks.replaceDataSource(dirpath(dirpath
                                (layerBlocks.dataSource)),
                            'FILEGDB_WORKSPACE',
                            basepath(selectedBlock))
if layerStops.dataSource != selectedBusStop:
    layerStops.replaceDataSource(dirpath(dirpath
                                (layerStops.dataSource)),
                                    'FILEGDB_WORKSPACE',
                                    basepath(selectedBusStop))
if layerBuffer.dataSource != selectedStopBuffer:
  layerBuffer.replaceDataSource(dirpath( dirpath(
                                layerBuffer.dataSource)),
                            'FILEGDB_WORKSPACE',
                            basepath(selectedStopBuffer))
```

If statements are used to check whether the data sources are correct. If not, they are replaced with the correct data sources using the replaceDataSource() layer method. This method requires three parameters: the workspace (in this case, the File Geodatabase), the workspace type, and the name of the new feature class data source, which must be in the same workspace for the replaceDataSource() method to work (though it does not need to be in the same feature dataset).

Adjusting layer visibility

The layer objects have a property that allows us to adjust their visibility. Setting this Boolean property to True or False will adjust the layer's visibility on (True) or off (False):

```
layerStops.visible = True
layerBuffer.visible = True
layerCensus.visible = False
```

We want the layer variable layerCensus, which is the new blocks_lyr object, to be turned off, so it is set to False, but the bus stops and buffer layer objects need to be visible, so they are set to True.

Generating a buffer from the bus stops feature class

All of the variables have been generated or assigned, so the next step is to use a `SearchCursor` to search through the selected bus stops. For each bus stop, buffer objects will be generated to find census blocks that intersect with these individual bus stops:

```
with arcpy.da.SearchCursor(Bus_Stops,['SHAPE@','STOPID','NAME',
                            'BUS_SIGNAG' ,'OID@',
                            'SHAPE@XY'],sql) as cursor:

    for row in cursor:

        stopPointGeometry = row[0]

        stopBuffer = stopPointGeometry.buffer(bufferDist)

        with arcpy.da.UpdateCursor(layerBlocks,['OID@']) as
dcursor:

            for drow in dcursor:

                dcursor.deleteRow()
```

For each row of data retrieved from the Bus Stops feature class, a number of attributes are returned, contained in a tuple. The first of these, row[0], is a `PointGeometry` object. This object has a buffer method that is used to generate a buffer `Polygon` object in memory, which is then assigned to the `stopBuffer` variable. Once the buffer object is created, the data access UpdateCursor's `deleteRow()` method is used to erase the rows in the census blocks layer. Once the rows have been deleted, the layer can then be repopulated with newly selected census blocks that will be identified in the next section.

Intersecting the bus stop buffer and census blocks

To identify the census blocks intersecting with the buffer around each bus stop, the ArcToolbox tool SelectLayerByLocation is invoked using the ArcPy method `SelectLayerByLocation_management()`:

```
arcpy.SelectLayerByLocation_management('blocks_lyr', 'intersect',
                            stopBuffer, "", "NEW_SELECTION")
        with arcpy.da.SearchCursor('blocks_lyr', ['SHAPE@',
                            'POP10','OID@']) as bcursor:

                inCursor = arcpy.da.InsertCursor(selectedBlock,
                                        ['SHAPE@', 'POP10'])
```

```
        for drow in bcursor:
            data = drow[0],drow[1]
            inCursor.insertRow(data)
    del inCursor
```

This method requires the in-memory `blocks_lyr` layer object and the newly created buffer object assigned to the variable `stopBuffer`. It also requires the type of selection `intersect` and another parameter that controls whether the selection will be added to an existing selection or will be a new selection. In this case, we want a new selection, as only the census blocks that intersect the current bus stop are needed.

Once the census blocks have been selected and identified, the shape data and population data is passed to the feature class represented by the variable `selectedBlock` using an `InsertCursor`. The InsertCursor must be deleted using the del keyword, as only one `InsertCursor` or `UpdateCursor` can be in memory at a time.

Populating the selected bus stop and buffer feature classes

In a similar manner, the next step is to populate the bus stop and buffer feature classes that will be used in the map production. The bus stops feature class is first made blank using the `deleteRow()` method, and then the selected bus stop shape field data is inserted into the feature class. The same steps are then taken with the bus stop buffers feature class and the buffer geometry object:

```
with arcpy.da.UpdateCursor(selectedBusStop,['OID@']) as dcursor:
    for drow in dcursor:
        dcursor.deleteRow()
inBusStopCursor = arcpy.da.InsertCursor(selectedBusStop,['SHAPE@'])
data = [row[0]]
inBusStopCursor.insertRow(data)
del inBusStopCursor
with arcpy.da.UpdateCursor(selectedStopBuffer,['OID@']) as dcursor:
    for drow in dcursor:
        dcursor.deleteRow()
inBufferCursor = arcpy.da.InsertCursor(selectedStopBuffer,
                                       ['SHAPE@'])
data = [stopBuffer]
```

```
inBufferCursor.insertRow(data)

del inBufferCursor
```

Updating the text elements

Now that the data has been generated and written to the feature classes created to hold them, the next step is to update the layout elements. This includes layer properties that will affect the legend, the extent of the data frame, and the text elements:

```
layerStops.name = "Stop #{0}".format(row[1])

dataFrame.extent = arcpy.Extent(row[-1][0]-1200,row[-1][1]-1200,
                                row[-1][0]+1200,row[-1][1]-1200)

subTitleText.text = "Route {0}".format(row[2])

titleText.text = "Bus Stop {0}".format(row[1])

arcpy.RefreshActiveView()
```

The name of the bus stops layer is adjusted using its name property to reflect the current bus stop. The data frame extent is adjusted by creating an `arcpy.Extent` object and passing it four parameters: *Xmin, Ymin, Xmax, Ymax*. To generate these values I have used the somewhat arbitrary value of 1200 feet to create a square around the bus stop. The text elements are updated using their text property. Finally, the `RefreshActiveView()` method is used to ensure that the map document window is correctly updated to the new extent.

Exporting the adjusted map to PDF

The final step is to pass the newly adjusted map document object to ArcPy's `ExportToPDF` method. This method requires two parameters, the map document object and a string that represents the file path of the PDF:

```
outPath = pdfFolder.format(str(row[1])+"_"+ str(row[-2]))+'.pdf'

arcpy.mapping.ExportToPDF(mxdObject,outPath)

titleText.text = 'Title Element'

subTitleText.text = 'Subtitle Element'

arcpy.RefreshActiveView()
```

The PDF file path string is generated from the pdfFolder string template and the ID of the bus stop, along with the object ID and the file extension `.pdf`. Once that and the map document object represented by the variable mxdObject are passed to the `ExportToPDF` method, the PDF will be generated. The text elements are then reset and the view is refreshed to ensure that the map document will be ready for the next time the script is used.

Running the script in the Python Window

Open up the map document called `MapAdjust.mxd` if it is not open already. Open the **Python** Window and right click in the window. Select **Load** from the menu. When the file dialog opens, find the script called `Chapter8_6_AdjustmapCURRENT.py` and select it, making sure that the file paths within it are correct. Push **OK** and it will load in the Python Window. Push **Enter** once the script is loaded to run the script. It can take a few seconds or more for it to be obvious that the script is running.

> Note that the Python Window is not a great place to execute ArcPy scripts in most cases, as it is somewhat limited when compared to IDEs. Using it to load and execute a script that performs these map document adjustments is one of the best uses of the Python Window.

Once the script is running, the adjustments to the map document will begin to appear and repeat. This is a fascinating process, as the effects of running the script are visible in a manner that is not readily available when running Python scripts. Once the PDFs begin to be generated, open one up to view the output. The script will generate a map for each bus stop on the selected bus line, so feel free to shut down the map document after generating a set number of the PDFs.

Here is an example of the output:

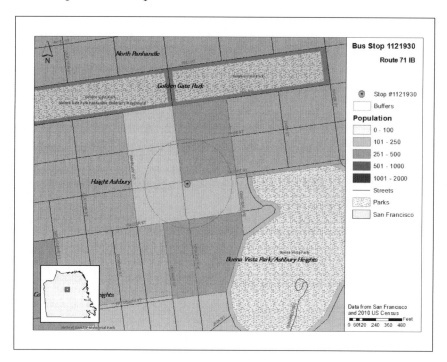

The maps generated by the script show each bus stop at the center, surrounded by the buffer and the symbolized census blocks with which the buffer intersects. The title, subtitle and the legend have been adjusted to indicate the bus stop depicted in the map. With ArcPy, we are now in control of both the parts of geospatial analysis: the analysis itself, and the cartographic production depicting the result of the output.

Summary

In this chapter arcpy.mapping was introduced and used to control the elements of map documents that need to be adjusted to create custom maps. By joining geospatial analysis and map production together, we are closer to utilizing the full power of ArcPy.

In the next chapter, we will go further with arcpy.mapping and create a script tool that can be added to ArcToolbox, which will run the analysis as well as generate maps from the resulting data. We will also refine the script and introduce Data Driven Pages to discuss how that powerful tool can be used in an ArcPy script.

9

More ArcPy.Mapping Techniques

The ability to control map document cartography, while also running geospatial analyses, increases the power and usefulness of ArcPy. The properties and methods of `arcpy.mapping` can be utilized to manipulate layer objects, map scales and data frame extents, or even to set definition queries. By combining automated geospatial analysis with dynamic map production, scripted mapping systems are made possible. This chapter will cover the following topics:

- Arcpy.mapping Layer objects
- Layer object definition queries and extents
- Arcpy.mapping Data Frame objects
- Creating dynamically scaled maps

Using arcpy.mapping to control Layer objects

`Arcpy.mapping` Layer objects are used to control the properties of layers within map document data frames. Turning layer visibility on and off, adding new layers, and adjusting layer order can all be accomplished using Layer object properties.

Creating Layer objects involves passing parameters to the `arcpy.mapping.`
`ListLayers()` method. As discussed in *Chapter 8, Introduction to ArcPy.Mapping*,
when referencing an `arcpy.mapping.MapDocument` object, the layers within the map
document can be accessed using zero-based indexing. This code will print the list of
Layer objects contained within the data frame called Layers in an MXD:

```
import arcpy
mxdPath = r'C:\Projects\MXDs\Chapter9\MapDocument1.mxd'
mxdObject = arcpy.mapping.MapDocument(mxdPath)
dataFrame = arcpy.mapping.ListDataFrames(mxdObject, "Layers")[0]
layersList = arcpy.mapping.ListLayers(mxdObject,"",dataFrame)
print layersList
```

The layers within the data frame called **Layers**, have been assigned to the variable
`layersList` using the `ListLayers()` method. Each layer in `layersList` can be
accessed using zero-based indexing. Once the layers have been accessed within the
list and either assigned to a variable or placed inside a `for` loop, the properties and
methods of the Layer objects can be utilized.

> The second parameter of the `ListLayers` method is empty here,
> but does not have to be. It is a wild card parameter that will limit the
> returned Layer objects to those that match the pattern of the wild card.
> For instance, ***Stops** would return all layers with the name **Stops** at the
> end. Multiple asterisks can be used to find layers with the word at the
> beginning, middle, or end of the layer name.

Layer object methods and properties

Layer object properties and methods can either be read only, meaning they can be
checked but not adjusted, or they are read and write, meaning they can be adjusted
within the script. Let's explore a number of these properties and methods, and see
how they can be used to control the look and feel of the maps produced from the
map document, as well as the data from the script analysis.

Definition queries

An important property of Layer objects is the ability to dynamically set definition queries. A definition query is a SQL statement `where` clause that limits the data available for display, query, or other data operations (buffers, intersections, etc.) to only the rows that match the `where` clause. Definition queries could be set in an MXD by opening a layer's properties menu and using the Definition Query tab, but here we are concerned with how to add them programmatically. Following is an example of how to do this:

```
layersList = arcpy.mapping.ListLayers(mxdObject,"",dataFrame)

busStops = layersList[0]

busStops.definitionQuery = "NAME = '71 IB' AND BUS_SIGNAG = 'Ferry
Plaza'"
```

This valuable property can be utilized to reformat the code from *Chapter 8, Introduction to ArcPy.Mapping*. Remember the complicated second portion of the `Chapter8_6.py` script, where each bus stop along the `71 Inbound` line is selected and its geometry is written to another feature class? Instead, we can use Layer objects and definition queries to perform the same type of geometry operation. Let's examine how the first part of that operation (selecting the bus stop geometry and creating a buffer around it) looks when a definition query is used:

```
import arcpy

bufferDist = 400

mxdPath = r'C:\Projects\MXDs\Chapter9\MapDocument1.mxd'

mxdObject = arcpy.mapping.MapDocument(mxdPath)

dataFrame= arcpy.mapping.ListDataFrames(mxdObject, "Layers")[0]

layersList = arcpy.mapping.ListLayers(mxdObject,"",dataFrame)

busStops = layersList[0]

defQuery = "NAME = '71 IB' AND BUS_SIGNAG = 'Ferry Plaza'"

busStops.definitionQuery = defQuery

idList =[]

with arcpy.da.SearchCursor(busStops,['OID@']) as cursor:
    for row in cursor:
        idList.append(row[0])

for oid in idList:
    newQuery = "OBJECTID = {0}".format(oid)
  print newQuery
  busStops.definitionQuery = newQuery
```

```
    with arcpy.da.SearchCursor(busStops,['SHAPE@','STOPID','NAME',
                                         'BUS_SIGNAG','OID@','SHAPE@XY'])
                                         as cursor:

        for row in cursor:

            stopPointGeometry = row[0]

            stopBuffer = stopPointGeometry.buffer(bufferDist)
```

In this example, the definition query is used to limit the potential results from the SearchCursor to the bus stop specified by the query. However, this is overly cumbersome and the definition query doesn't add much, as first another SearchCursor is needed to extract the ObjectID information from the busStops layer. This complicates the code when only one SearchCursor is necessary.

Definition queries should be used to select the blocks that intersect with the buffer, as this will eliminate the need to use the complicated Search Cursor and Insert Cursor setup that was employed in *Chapter 8, Introduction to ArcPy.Mapping*. Let's reformulate the code so that definition queries are properly used on the census block Layer object.

The first step is to add some code that will generate the SQL statement that will be used as the definition query:

```
import arcpy
bufferDist = 400
mxdPath = r'C:\Projects\MXDs\Chapter9\MapDocument1.mxd'
mxdObject = arcpy.mapping.MapDocument(mxdPath)
dataFrame = arcpy.mapping.ListDataFrames(mxdObject,
                                         "Layers")[0]
layersList = arcpy.mapping.ListLayers(mxdObject,
                                      "",dataFrame)
busStops = layersList[0]
censusBlocks = layersList[3]
sql = "NAME = '71 IB' AND BUS_SIGNAG = 'Ferry Plaza'"
with arcpy.da.SearchCursor(busStops,['SHAPE@',
                                     'STOPID',
                                     'NAME',
                                     'BUS_SIGNAG',
                                     'OID@'],sql) as cursor:

    for row in cursor:

            bus Query = 'OBJECTID = {0}'.format(row[-1])

            busStops.definitionQuery = bus Query
```

```
stopPointGeometry = row[0]
stop Buffer = stopPointGeometry. Buffer(bufferDist)
arcpy.SelectLayerByLocation_management(censusBlocks,
                                'intersect',
                                stopBuffer,
                                "",
                                "NEW_SELECTION")
blockList = []
with arcpy.da.SearchCursor(censusBlocks,
                        ['OID@']) as bcursor:
    for brow in bcursor:
        blockList.append(brow[0])
newQuery = 'OBJECTID IN ('
for COUNTER, oid in enumerate(blockList):
    if COUNTER < len(blockList)-1:
        newQuery += str(oid) + ','
    else:
        newQuery += str(oid)+ ')'
print newQuery
```

In this section, the code assigns the census blocks layer in the MXD to the variable censusBlocks. The bus stops SearchCursor is then created, and the 400 foot buffer is generated for each row to select the census blocks surrounding the bus stop. Once the correct blocks have been selected, a second SearchCursor is used on the censusBlocks Layer object to find the ObjectID (using the OID@ token) of the selected blocks. The ObjectIDs are then appended to the list called blockList.

This list is then iterated in a for loop to generate a string SQL statement. Using the initial string assigned to the variable newQuery, the for loop will add the ObjectIDs of each select block to the string to create a valid SQL statement. The for loop uses the function enumerate to count the number of loops that the for loop performs; this allows for an if/then statement to be used. The if/then statement determines what comes after the ObjectID in the string, as each ObjectID must be separated by a comma, except for the final ObjectID, which must be followed by the closing parenthesis. The for loop produces a SQL statement similar to this example:

```
OBJECTID IN (910,1664,1812,1813,2725,6382)
```

The `print` statement at the end is used to demonstrate the results of this section of the code, and also to give that warm fuzzy feeling that comes from seeing the results of the code working. Once we are sure that the code is generating valid SQL statements (closed parenthesis and comma separated `ObjectIDs`), the next step is to assign the definition query to the `censusBlocks` Layer object and use the result to generate a map of the area.

Controlling the data frame window extent and scale

In *Chapter 8, Introduction to ArcPy.Mapping* we started to explore the properties and methods of the data frame. Using the `arcpy.Extent` object, we were able to set the extent of the data frame to an extent that was hard-coded into the script. However, this does not always capture the entire extent of large census blocks. Using a combination of definition queries and the data frame extent and scale properties, we can avoid these unwanted results.

There are two data frame object methods used to shift the data frame window to the area of interest, in this case the selected census blocks. The first, which we are not using here, is `dataFrame.zoomToSelectedFeatures`. The second, is to assign the data frame's extent property to the extent of the census block layer after the definition query has been assigned to it.

I prefer the second method, as it will work even when there is no selected census blocks. Also, as the maps that are produced by this script should not show the selection of the blocks, we will have to add code to explicitly clear the selection once the correct census blocks have been identified:

```
censusBlocks.definitionQuery = newQuery
dataFrame.extent = censusBlocks.getExtent()
arcpy.SelectLayerByAttribute_management(censusBlocks,
                          "CLEAR_SELECTION")
```

The definition query has made it easy to move the data frame window to the area of interest, as the extent rectangle (or envelope) of the layer is now only around the specified blocks and the `dataFrame` extent property can be set to the extent rectangle. However, this is not always cartographically desirable as it seems better to move the data frame window back from the extent rectangle. To do that, we'll access the data frame the object's scale property.

The scale property can be set to be a multiplier of the current scale to avoid hard-coding any specific distances when adjusting the data frame extent. When using the scale property, it is important to remember to use the `arcpy.RefreshActiveView()` method, as it will refresh the data frame window to the new scale.

```
dataFrame.scale = dataFrame.scale * 1.1

arcpy.RefreshActiveView()
```

As the data frame extent was set in the few lines before this, the current scale represents the envelope of the selected census blocks. To adjust it, assess the property and apply a multiplier. In this case, the multiplier is 1.1, but it could be any value. This makes the resulting map look better by giving the analysis results some background context.

Adding a Layer object

The last step before exporting out the maps is to add the 400 foot buffers created above as a layer to the data frame object. To accomplish this, we need to create a symbolized layer ahead of time and copy its symbology to ensure it looks as desired. This will be added to the **MXD** as a placeholder layer, and assigned to the `bufferLayer` variable in the script.

1. Open up an **MXD** and add the **bus stop feature class**.

2. Run the **Buffer Tool** in the **Proximity** toolset in the **Analysis** toolset of the **ArcToolbox**, adding the **bus stop feature class** as the input and setting the buffer size to **400 feet**. After the tool has run, open the properties of the buffer layer and symbolize the layer as desired.

3. Once the layer has been symbolized, right-click on the layer and select **Save As Layer File**.

4. Save the layer in a folder and close the **MXD**.

5. Open up the **MapDocument1.mxd** map document and add the layer using the **Add Data** button.

6. Make sure to change the name to **400 Foot Buffer** and to add it to the legend above the **Population** section.

7. In the script, assign the buffer layer to the variable `bufferLayer`.

8. Lower in the script, in the bus stop `SearchCursor`, add these lines below where the buffer is generated around the bus stop geometry:

```
arcpy.CopyFeatures_management(stopBuffer,
r"C:\Projects\Output\400Buffer.shp")
```

```
bufferLayer.replaceDataSource(r"C:\Projects\Output","SHAPEFILE_
WORKSP
ACE","400Buffer")
```

These two lines copy the buffer generated to disk as a shapefile and then replace the data source of the `bufferLayer` Layer object with the newly created buffer. Note that the name of the shapefile does not include the `.shp` extension; the `SHAPEFILE_WORKSPACE` parameter makes this unnecessary.

To make sure that each new buffer shapefile can be written over an existing shapefile, add the following line below the `import arcpy` line to make sure that files can be overwritten:

```
arcpy.env.overwriteOutput = 1
```

Exporting the maps

The final step of this script is to export the maps of the area surrounding each bus stop. To do this, we will borrow some code from the script `Chapter8_6_AdjustMap.py` and add the whole script to a file called `Chapter9.py`. This code will identify and adjust the title and subtitle elements, making it possible to customize each resulting PDF:

```
import arcpy
arcpy.env.overwriteOutput = 1
bufferDist = 400
pdfFolder = r'C:\Projects\PDFs\Chapter9\Map_{0}'
mxdPath = r'C:\Projects\MXDs\Chapter9\MapDocument1.mxd'
mxdObject = arcpy.mapping.MapDocument(mxdPath)
dataFrame = arcpy.mapping.ListDataFrames(mxdObject,
                                         "Layers")[0]
elements = arcpy.mapping.ListLayoutElements(mxdObject)
for el in elements:
    if el.type =="TEXT_ELEMENT":
        if el.text == 'Title Element':
            titleText = el
```

```
        elif el.text == 'Subtitle Element':
            subTitleText = el
layersList = arcpy.mapping.ListLayers(mxdObject,
                                "",dataFrame)


busStops = layersList[0]
bufferLayer = layersList[2]
censusBlocks = layersList[4]
sql = "NAME = '71 IB' AND BUS_SIGNAG = 'Ferry Plaza'"
with arcpy.da.SearchCursor(busStops,['SHAPE@',
                                'STOPID',
                                'NAME',
                                'BUS_SIGNAG',
                                'OID@'],sql) as cursor:
    for row in cursor:
        busQuery = 'OBJECTID = {0}'.format(row[-1])
        busStops.definitionQuery = busQuery
        stopPointGeometry = row[0]
        stopBuffer = stopPointGeometry.buffer(bufferDist)
        arcpy.CopyFeatures_management(stopBuffer,r"C:\Projects\
                                Output\400Buffer.shp")
        bufferLayer.replaceDataSource(r"C:\Projects\Output",
                "SHAPEFILE_WORKSPACE",
              "400Buffer")
        arcpy.SelectLayerByLocation_management(censusBlocks,
                                        'intersect',
                                        stopBuffer,
                                        "",
                                        "NEW_SELECTION")
        blockList = []
        with arcpy.da.SearchCursor(censusBlocks,
                            ['OID@']) as bcursor:
            for brow in bcursor:
                blockList.append(brow[0])
        newQuery = 'OBJECTID IN ('
        for COUNTER, oid in enumerate(blockList):
```

```
        if COUNTER < len(blockList)-1:
            newQuery += str(oid) + ','
        else:
            newQuery += str(oid)+ ')'
    print newQuery
    censusBlocks.definitionQuery = newQuery
    dataFrame.extent = censusBlocks.getExtent()
    arcpy.SelectLayerByAttribute_management(censusBlocks,
                                    "CLEAR_SELECTION")
    dataFrame.scale = dataFrame.scale * 1.1
    arcpy.RefreshActiveView()
    subTitleText.text = "Route {0}".format(row[2])
    titleText.text = "Bus Stop {0}".format(row[1])
    outPath = pdfFolder.format( str(row[1])) + '.pdf'
    print outPath
    arcpy.mapping.ExportToPDF(mxdObject,outPath)
    titleText.text = 'Title Element'
    subTitleText.text = 'Subtitle Element'
    censusBlocks.definitionQuery = ''
    busStops.definitionQuery = ''
```

Summary

In this chapter, we covered the use of layer definition queries, data frame extents and scales, and layer source replacement to ease the production of maps. By using definition queries, the layers can be modified to new extents, making it easier to zoom into the layer extent and to set the scale of the data frame. The definition queries also limit which members of a layer are displayed within the data frame. Layer source replacement was used as a cartographic control, allowing us to pre-generate the style of a layer and adjust the data that it represented dynamically.

In the next chapter, we will combine the lessons from the last three chapters, allowing us to create a script tool that will run analysis and produce spreadsheets and maps from the analysis results.

10
Advanced Geometry Object Methods

In this chapter, we will discuss advanced Geometry object methods, previously discussed in *Chapter 6, Working with ArcPy Geometry Objects*. The goal of this book is to give an introduction to ArcPy and its modules, while also demonstrating how to apply these tools when creating enduring GIS workflows. Performing an analysis once is good, but doing it over and over, with the click of a button, is better. Making the analysis results sharable in an industry standard format is also desirable. In the ArcGIS world, the best way to do this is with ArcPy and script tools that take advantage of Geometry object methods.

This chapter will cover the following topics:

- Adding common functions to a module in the Python path
- Making the analysis more advanced by adding point generation
- Advanced Polygon object methods
- Using the XLWT to create Excel spreadsheets

Creating a Python module

An important step towards creating reusable code is to package its component functions into a module that can be called from the Python path by any script. To start, we need to create a folder in the site-packages folder where Python modules are placed when downloaded and extracted using the Python module process, or when running the setup.py script included with shared modules.

Modules package together functions in one or more scripts into a folder that can be shared with others (though they often depend on other modules to run). We have used some of the built-in modules such as the csv module and third-party modules such as ArcPy. Let's explore their construction to get a feel of how a module is packaged for use and sharing.

> Many modules are not placed within the site-packages folder, but they require the Python path to be modified to make them **importable**. Placing modules within the site-packages folder eliminates this requirement.

Open up the site-packages folder in Windows Explorer by navigating to C:\Python27\ArcGIS10.2\Lib\site-packages (or C:\Python27\Lib\site-packages if you're using the standard Python 2.7 installation) folder. Once in the folder, create a new folder called **common**, as shown in the following screenshot:

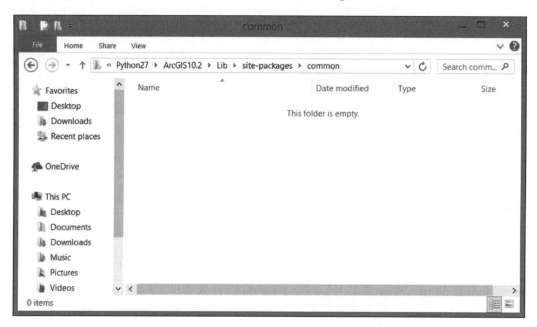

The __init__.py file

Within this folder, a special file needs to be added to let Python recognize the folder as a module. This file, called __init__.py, takes advantage of the special property of Python called magic objects or attributes that are built into Python. These magic objects use the leading and trailing double underscore to avoid any confusion with custom functions.

Note that these are *double* underscores; single underscores are usually used for so-called private functions within custom Python classes.

The __init__.py file is used to indicate that the folder is a module (making it importable using the import keyword), and to initiate the module by calling any modules that it may in turn rely on. However, there is no requirement to add import commands to the __init__.py file; it can be an empty file and will still perform the module recognition functionality that we require.

1. Open up **IDLE** or **Aptana** or your favorite IDE, and in the folder called **common**, add a new Python file and call it __init__.py. This file will remain empty for now.

2. Now that we have initiated the module, we need to create a script that will hold our common functions. Let's call it useful.py because these functions will be most useful for this analysis and others.

3. The next step is to transfer functions that we had created in earlier chapters. These valuable functions are locked into those scripts, so by adding them to useful.py, we will make them available to all other scripts we craft.

One important function is the formatSQLMultiple from *Chapter 4, Complex ArcPy Scripts and Generalizing Functions,* which generates SQL statements using a template and a list of data. By adding it to useful.py, we will be able to call the function anytime a SQL statement is required.

4. Open the script Chapter4Modified2.py and copy the function, and then paste it into useful.py. It has no dependencies, so it does not have to be modified.

Another useful function from that script is the formatIntersect function that generates a string of file paths that are used when running the ArcToolbox Intersect tool. While we have reached deeper into ArcPy since that function was designed, and no longer need to call the Intersect tool in our bus stop analysis, it does not mean that we will never need to call it in the future. It is still useful and should be added to useful.py.

The last function that we can raid is the createCSV() function. Copy and paste it from Chapter4Modified.py into useful.py. However, to avoid the need to import the CSV module separately, we will need to modify the function slightly. Here is how it should look:

```python
def createCSV(data, csvname, mode ='ab'):
    'creates a csv file'
    import csv
    with open(csvname, mode) as csvfile:
        csvwriter = csv.writer(csvfile, delimiter=',')
        csvwriter.writerow(data)
    del csv
```

By importing and then deleting the csv module, we are able to use it to generate the csv file and then remove the module from memory using the del keyword.

Now that we have the functions we will be reusing saved in the useful.py script, inside the common module, let's explore how to call them using Python's import method. Open up a Python executable, using either Python.exe or IDLE, or the built-in terminal in Aptana. At the triple chevron prompt (**>>>**), write the following line:

```python
>>> from common.useful import createCSV
>>>
```

If the second triple chevron-shaped prompt appears, the function was correctly imported from the module. To import the functions in this module in a script, use the same import structure and list the functions desired, separating them using a comma:

```
from common.useful import createCSV, formatSQLMultiple
```

The functions in the script `useful.py` were called using Python dot notation. This is made possible because the `__init__.py` file indicates to Python that the folder `common` is now a module, and that it should expect a method called `useful` to be present, with the functions `createCSV` and `formatSQLMultiple` inside it.

Adding advanced analysis components

The bus stop analysis we have used to introduce ArcPy can be further extended to generate more refined results. To better estimate the true number of people that each bus stop serves, let's add a function that will generate random points within the blocks considered, while eliminating parks and other areas that do not contain housing.

To do this, we need to introduce a new data set from the `San Francisco` geodatabase, the `RPD_Parks` feature class. By using this feature class to reduce the area considered for our analysis, we can generate a more realistic assessment of the service area population for each bus stop.

While using the **ArcToolbox Erase tool** to erase the area represented in the `RPD_Parks` polygons would be a usual step when running a spatial analysis, there are drawbacks to this option. The first is that the **Erase** tool is only available with the ArcGIS for Desktop Advanced license level, making it available only to certain users. The second drawback is that the tool produces an intermediate data set, something to be avoided wherever possible.

Using ArcPy will give us the ability to avoid both of these drawbacks. We can create a script that will generate random points only within the fraction of the census block polygons that do not intersect with the `RPD_Parks` feature class. To do this, we will reach deeper into the methods of the ArcPy `Polygon` object.

Advanced Polygon object methods

In *Chapter 6, Working with ArcPy Geometry Objects* we started exploring the ArcPy Geometry objects and how to use their methods to perform in-memory spatial analysis. The **Buffer** and **Intersect** methods of these objects were introduced and used to generate analysis results. Next, we will discuss more of these methods and show how they can help improve in-memory spatial analysis.

The `Polygon` object has a method called `Difference` that allows us to find the area of non-intersection when two polygons intersect. Passing a `census block polygon` and a `park polygon` as parameters will return (as a polygon object) the fraction of the first parameter where no overlap occurs. Another important method is called `Overlaps`, which is called to test whether two Geometry objects (points, lines, or polygons) intersect. If there is an overlap, the `Overlaps` method will return **True**, while returning **False** if there is no overlap between the two objects. `Union` is also an important method that will be used within this chapter, it allows for two Geometry objects to be **unioned** into one object.

Let's explore these important methods. To find the non-intersect area of two polygon objects, the following function combines the `Overlaps` and `Difference` methods:

```
def nonIntersect(poly1,poly2):
    'returns area of non-intersect between two polygons'
    if poly1.overlaps(poly2) == True:
        return poly1.difference(poly2)
```

The function `nonIntersect` accepts two `Polygon` objects as parameters. The first parameter, `poly1`, is the polygon of intersect (the census block polygon) and the second parameter, `poly2`, is the polygon to be checked for overlap. The if conditional uses the `Overlaps` method and returns **True** if there is an overlap between the two parameters. If there is any overlap, the `difference()` method returns the non-intersect area as a polygon object. However, this function should be extended to cover situations where the `Overlaps()` method returns False:

```
def nonIntersect(poly1,poly2):
    'returns area of non-intersect between two polygons'
    if poly1.overlaps(poly2) == True:
        return poly1.difference(poly2)
    else:
        return poly1
```

The function will now return the first parameter when the `Overlaps` method returns `False`, indicating that there is no overlap between the two polygon objects. This function is now complete and available to be used in an analysis. Because `nonIntersect()` is a function that can be used in other spatial analyses, copy it and add it to `useful.py`.

Generating random points to represent population

The next step to improve the bus stop analysis is to generate points to represent the population of each census block. While random points will not provide a perfect representation of the population, it will serve as a good model of the population and allow us to avoid area averaging to find the rough population of each census block served by a bus stop. The CreateRandomPoints tool in the ArcToolbox Data Management toolset makes it simple to generate the points.

The CreateRandomPoints tool accepts a number of required and optional parameters. As the tool generates a feature class, the required parameters are the workspace where the feature class will be placed and the name of the feature class. The optional parameters of interest are the constraining feature class and the number of points to be generated. As we are looking to avoid creating new feature classes in the intermediate steps of our analysis, we can utilize the in_memory workspace, which allows feature classes to be generated in memory, meaning they are not written to the hard drive.

Because there is a need to generate a specific number of random points for each census block, we should create a function that will accept a constraining polygon and population figure that represents each census block. The in_memory workspace won't work for every situation, however, so we'll provide the workspace parameter with a default value:

```
def generatePoints(fc, pop,constrant, workspace='in_memory'):
    'generate random points'
    import os, arcpy
    arcpy.CreateRandomPoints_management(workspace, fc,
constrant, "", pop, "")
    return os.path.join(workspace, fc)
```

The function will create the feature class in the workspace desired and will return the path (joined using the os module) to the feature class for use in the rest of the script. This function is also reusable and should be copied into useful.py.

Using the functions within a script

Now that we have created the functions that will help us to run a more advanced spatial analysis, let's add them to a script along with some SearchCursors to iterate through the data:

```
# Import the necessary modules
import arcpy, os
from common.useful import nonIntersect, generatePoints,createCSV


# Add an overwrite statement
arcpy.env.overwriteOutput = True


# Define the data inputs
busStops = r'C:\Projects\SanFrancisco.gdb\SanFrancisco\Bus_Stops'
parks = r'C:\Projects\SanFrancisco.gdb\SanFrancisco\RPD_Parks'
censusBlocks = r'C:\Projects\SanFrancisco.gdb\SanFrancisco\
CensusBlocks2010'
csvName = r'C:\Projects\Output\Chapter10Analysis.csv'


# Create the spreadsheet in memory and add field headers
headers = 'Line Name','Stop ID', 'Total Population Served'
createCSV(headers,csvName,mode='wb')


# Copy the census block data into a feature layer
arcpy.MakeFeatureLayer_management(censusBlocks,'census_lyr')


# Copy the park data geometries into a list and union them allparkGeoms =
arcpy.CopyFeatures_management(parks,arcpy.Geometry())
parkUnion = parkGeoms[0]
for park in parkGeoms[1:]:
    parkUnion = parkUnion.union(park)


# Create a search cursor to iterate the bus stop data
sql = "NAME = '71 IB' AND BUS_SIGNAG = 'Ferry Plaza'"
with arcpy.da.SearchCursor(busStops, ['NAME','STOPID',
                                      'SHAPE@'],sql) as cursor:
    for row in cursor:
```

```
        lineName = row[0]
        stopID = row[1]
        stop = row[2]
        busBuf = stop.buffer(400)
        # Select census blocks that intersect the bus buffer
        arcpy.SelectLayerByLocation_management("census_lyr","intersect",
                                    busBuf,'','NEW_SELECTION')
        # Use a second Cursor to find the selected population
        totalPopulation = 0
        with arcpy.da.SearchCursor("census_lyr",['SHAPE@','POP10',
            'BLOCKID10']) as ncursor:
            for nrow in ncursor:
                block = nrow[0]
                checkedBlock = nonIntersect(block, parkUnion)
                blockName = nrow[2]
                population = nrow[1]
                if population != 0:
                    points = generatePoints("PopPoints",
                        population,checkedBlock)
            pointsGeoms = arcpy.CopyFeatures_management(points,
                                            arcpy.Geometry())
                    pointsUnion = pointsGeoms[0]
                    for point in pointsGeoms[1:]:
                        pointsUnion = pointsUnion.union(point)
                    pointsInBuffer=busBuf.intersect(pointsUnion, 1)
                    intersectedPoints = pointsInBuffer.pointCount
                    totalPopulation += intersectedPoints
        # Add the tallied data to the spreadsheet
        data = lineName, stopID, totalPopulation
        print 'data written', data
        createCSV(data, csvName)


#Start the spreadsheet to see the results

os.startfile(csvName)
```

Let's review the code, section by section, as that is a lot to take in at first.

The import portion is where we call the usual modules, arcpy and os, along with our custom functions in the common module:

```
import arcpy, os
from common.useful import nonIntersect
from common.useful import generatePoints
from common.useful import formatSQLMultiple
from common.useful import nonIntersectcreateCSV
```

As discussed previously, the functions in the common module's useful method are called using the Python dot notation and the from ... import ... importation style, making them available directly. Many functions can be imported on one line, separated by commas, or individually as shown here.

The next line, which sets the ArcPy Environment overwrite property to True, is very important because it allows us to overwrite the results of the Create random points operation. If the results were not overwritten, the function results, which otherwise would use all available memory and cause the script to fail:

```
arcpy.env.overwriteOutput = True
```

 It is important to be careful with this overwrite setting because it will allow for any feature class to be overwritten. All of our output is in memory and only generated for the analysis, so there is little need to worry here, but take care to make sure that nothing important is overwritten when running a script.

The next portion is the set of variables that will be used in this script, and will initiate the spreadsheet that will be used to collect the results of the analysis:

```
busStops = r'C:\PacktDB.gdb\SanFrancisco\Bus_Stops'
parks = r'C:\PacktDB.gdb\SanFrancisco\RPD_Parks'
censusBlocks = r'C:\PacktDB.gdb\SanFrancisco\CensusBlocks2010'
csvName = r'C:\Projects\Output\Chapter10Analysis.csv'
headers = 'Line Name','Stop ID', 'Total Population Served'
createCSV(headers,csvName,mode='wb')
```

The file paths assigned to variables here could be replaced with ArcPy parameters if we were to turn this into a script tool, but for now, the hard-coded paths are fine. Below the variables, the results spreadsheet is created and the column field headers are added.

It is worth noting that the spreadsheet is created using the wb mode. This mode of binary file opening, known as wb (write binary), is used for creating a new file. It must be explicitly passed into the createCSV() function as the default mode parameter is ab (append binary), which will create a new file if it does not exist, or add to one that already exists (a third binary mode is **rb** or **read binary**, which is used for opening an existing file).

The next few lines make data in the feature classes available in memory. The census block data is converted into a Feature Layer, while the RPD_Parks data is read into memory as a list of Polygon objects that is then unioned into a single, unified Polygon object called parkUnion:

```
arcpy.MakeFeatureLayer_management(censusBlocks,'census_lyr')
parkGeoms = arcpy.CopyFeatures_management(parks,
                    arcpy.Geometry())
parkUnion = parkGeoms[0]
for park in parkGeoms[1:]:
    parkUnion = parkUnion.union(park)
```

By using the CopyFeatures tool in the **Data Management** toolset, the parkGeoms variable is passed a list of the geometries for each row of data in the RPD_Parks feature class. However, we don't want to have to iterate through the park geometries to compare them to each census block, so the Union method is invoked to create one Polygon object from the entire list. By assigning the first member of the list to the parkUnion variable, and then iterating through the parkGeoms list to union the other geometries one by one, the result is one Polygon object that represents all parks within the RPD_Parks dataset.

Once all of the modules have been imported and the variables have been assigned, we can enter the for loop of the data access SearchCursor to begin the analysis. However, we don't want to run this for all of the bus stops, so we will use a SQL statement where clause, to limit the analysis to a single bus line:

```
sql = "NAME = '71 IB' AND BUS_SIGNAG = 'Ferry Plaza'"
with arcpy.da.SearchCursor(busStops, ['NAME','STOPID',
                                'SHAPE@'],sql) as cursor:

    for row in cursor:
        lineName = row[0]
        stopID = row[1]
        stop = row[2]
        busBuf = stop.buffer(400)
```

```
arcpy.SelectLayerByLocation_management("census_lyr",
                                       "intersect,busBuf,'',
                                       'NEW_SELECTION')

totalPopulation = 0
```

The first portion of the iteration involves entering the `for` loop and assigning the values of each row to a variable. A `Polygon` object buffer of `400` feet is created around the `PointGeometry` object returned by the `SearchCursor`. This buffer is then used to intersect with the census blocks `Feature Layer` to find and select all of the census blocks that intersect the buffer. To tally the population served by each buffer, the variable `totalPopulation` is created.

Once the selection has been performed, a second `SearchCursor` can be used to iterate through the selected blocks to retrieve their population values and `Polygon` objects for random point generation:

```
with arcpy.da.SearchCursor("census_lyr", ['SHAPE@', 'POP10',
               'BLOCKID10']) as ncursor:
    for nrow in ncursor:
            block = nrow[0]
            checkedBlock = nonIntersect(block, parkUnion)
            blockName = nrow[2]
            population = nrow[1]
```

In this iteration, once each census block has been retrieved (in the form of a Polygon object), the block is then checked against the **unioned** park geometry using the `nonIntersect` function created previously. This ensures that the points will only be created within areas that are not parks, that is, more likely to represent where people would live. The population values are also retrieved.

Once the constraining polygon (for example the census block) has been evaluated and any potential park portion has been removed, and the population value is available, the random points can be generated using the `generatePoints()` function:

```
if population != 0:
    points = generatePoints("PopPoints",population,checkedBlock)
    pointsGeoms = arcpy.CopyFeatures_management(points,arcpy.Geometry())
```

```
pointsUnion = pointsGeoms[0]
for point in pointsGeoms[1:]:
    pointsUnion = pointsUnion.union(point)
pointsInBuffer = busBuf.intersect(pointsUnion,1)
intersectedPoints = pointsInBuffer.pointCount
totalPopulation += intersectedPoints
```

The generatePoints() function requires three parameters. The first is the name of the feature class to be generated; this will be overwritten each time it is generated, thus avoiding the overuse of memory by creating an in_memory feature class for each census block. The other two parameters are the population value and the constraining Polygon object.

Once these have been passed to the function, it returns a file path to the newly created feature class and assigns the file path to the variable points. The geometries in points are then extracted using the CopyFeatures tool and assigned to the variable points. The Union method is again used to create a single, unified population PointGeometry object that will be intersected with the bus stop buffer. Once this intersection has been run, the resulting geometries are assigned to the pointsInBuffer variable and the pointCount method is used to find the number of points that were generated within the buffered area. This is our estimate of population within the census block, and this value is added to the totalPopulation variable to eventually yield the total estimated population within 400 feet of the bus stop.

The final lines of the script demonstrate how the data is collected into a tuple and passed to the createCSV() module to be written to our final spreadsheet:

```
data = lineName, stopID,totalPopulation
print 'data written', data
createCSV(data, csvName)
os.startfile(csvName)
```

The last line, `os.startfile(csvName)`, uses the `startfile` method of the `os` module to automatically open the spreadsheet once the analysis is completed. In this case, the spreadsheet `C:\Projects\Output\Chapter10Analysis.csv` has been populated with the results of the analysis and is opened to display these results. However, the user may have to indicate that the lines are comma separated values to open the script.

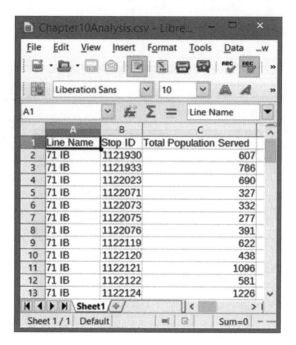

Instead of creating a comma separated value, we can take advantage of another Python module that is installed when ArcGIS 10.2 and ArcPy is installed. This module, called XLWT, is used to generate Excel spreadsheets, and along with the Excel spreadsheet reading module XLRD, is one of the most useful modules available to users of Python.

Creating an XLS using XLWT

XLWT is a powerful module that allows for a multitude of styling options. However, for our purposes we can ignore those options and create a function that will generate a spreadsheet with the results of our spatial analysis. This function can of course be added to `common.useful`:

```
def generateXLS(indatas, sheetName, fileName):

    import xlwt

    workbook = xlwt.Workbook()
```

```
sheet = workbook.add_sheet(sheetName)
for YCOUNTER, data in enumerate(indatas):
    for XCOUNTER, value in enumerate(data):
        sheet.write(YCOUNTER, XCOUNTER, value)
workbook.save(fileName)
```

This function requires three parameters, `indatas`- a list containing rows of iterable data, a string sheet name, and a string file name that ends with the `.xls` extension.

To use this function, add it to `common.useful`. Once it has been added, copy and rename the older analysis script so that it can be adjusted:

```
import arcpy, os
from common.useful import nonIntersect, generatePoints, generateXLS


arcpy.env.overwriteOutput = True


busStops = r'C:\Projects\PacktDB.gdb\SanFrancisco\Bus_Stops'
parks = r'C:\Projects\PacktDB.gdb\SanFrancisco\RPD_Parks'
censusBlocks =
r'C:\Projects\PacktDB.gdb\SanFrancisco\CensusBlocks2010'
xlsName = r'C:\Projects\Output\Chapter10Analysis.xls'


headers = 'Line Name','Stop ID', 'Total Population Served'
indatas = [headers]


arcpy.MakeFeatureLayer_management(censusBlocks,'census_lyr')parkGeoms =
arcpy.CopyFeatures_management(parks,arcpy.Geometry())
parkUnion = parkGeoms[0]
for park in parkGeoms[1:]:
    parkUnion = parkUnion.union(park)



sql = "NAME = '71 IB' AND BUS_SIGNAG = 'Ferry Plaza'"
with arcpy.da.SearchCursor(busStops, ['NAME','STOPID',
            'SHAPE@'],sql) as cursor:
    for row in cursor:
        lineName = row[0]
        stopID = row[1]
```

```
            stop = row[2]
            busBuf = stop.buffer(400)
            arcpy.SelectLayerByLocation_management("census_lyr","intersect",
                                                busBuf,'','NEW_SELECTION')
            totalPopulation = 0
            with arcpy.da.SearchCursor("census_lyr", ['SHAPE@','POP10',
                    'BLOCKID10']) as ncursor:
                for nrow in ncursor:
                    block = nrow[0]
                    checkedBlock = nonIntersect(block, parkUnion)
                    blockName = nrow[2]
                    population = nrow[1]
                    if population != 0:
                        points = generatePoints("PopPoints",
                                            population,checkedBlock)


    pointsGeoms = arcpy.CopyFeatures_management(points,
                                            arcpy.Geometry())
                    pointsUnion = pointsGeoms[0]
                    for point in pointsGeoms[1:]:
                        pointsUnion = pointsUnion.union(point)
                    pointsInBuffer = busBuf.intersect(pointsUnion,1)
                    intersectedPoints = pointsInBuffer.pointCount
                    totalPopulation += intersectedPoints
            data = lineName, stopID, totalPopulation
            indatas.append(data)
generateXLS(indatas, "Results", xlsName)
os.startfile(xlsName)
```

We can now generate Excel spreadsheets just as easily as we have generated CSV files while employing a reusable function. We now have the ability to perform repeatable spatial analysis fast and can produce results in industry standard formats.

Summary

In this chapter, we have explored how to create modules and reusable functions that will save scripting time in the future by allowing us to avoid rewriting these useful functions. We further explored the methods available through ArcPy Geometry objects, including the `Intersect`, `Overlaps`, and `Union` methods. We created a spatial analysis that writes no feature classes to disk, making it so that the analysis time is reduced and unnecessary files are avoided. Finally, we explored how to generate Excel spreadsheets using the `XLWT` module so that analysis results can be shared in industry standard formats.

In the next chapter, we will explore how to use ArcPy to interact with the ArcGIS for desktop extensions such as Network Analyst and Spatial Analyst. By incorporating their functionality within a script, we further increase our ability to create fast and repeatable spatial analysis workflows.

11
Network Analyst and Spatial Analyst with ArcPy

Use of the ArcGIS for Desktop extensions also benefits from the power of Python and ArcPy. The ability to model routes using a streets dataset or a bus routes dataset using ArcPy will help us convert entire workflows into script tools. Both Network Analysts and Spatial Analysts have access modules built into ArcPy for improved control of their available tools, methods, and properties.

This chapter will cover the following topics:

- Creating a simple network dataset
- Checking out the extensions
- The ArcPy Network Analyst module
- The ArcPy Spatial Analyst module

The Network Analyst extension

The ESRI's Network Analyst extension is a powerful tool to enable routing and network connectivity functionality within ArcGIS. The extension, when used for street routing, allows users to find the quickest path between two points along a road network. The route can be constrained by a number of factors, such as traffic or left turns, to better model road travel. Similar analysis can be run using other types of networks, such as water pipe networks or electrical networks.

Using Network Analyst

To use the Network Analyst extension, the ArcGIS for Desktop Advanced license is required. In ArcCatalog or ArcMap, click on the **Customize** menu and select **Extensions**. Once the Extensions menu is open, click on the checkbox next to turn on the **Network Analyst Extension.**

Creating a Feature Dataset

The first step to using a network dataset is to create one within a feature dataset. To do so, we will generate a feature dataset to hold the data of interest. Right-click on the **File** geodatabase that houses the **Bus Stop** data and select **New**, and then select **Feature Dataset** from the **New** menu. Name it `Chapter11Results` and click on **Next**.

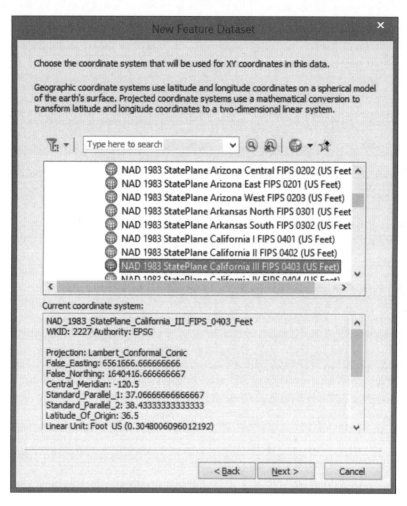

Next, select the **Spatial Reference System (SRS)**. In this case, we will be using the SRS of the local State Plane zone for San Francisco. It is a projected coordinate system, so select that folder, and then click on the `State Plane` folder. Once it is opened, select the folder called **NAD 1983(US Feet)**. From the available reference systems, select the one called **NAD 1983 StatePlane California III FIPS 0403 (US Feet)**. Click on **Next** to go to the next menu.

> This system is also known as 2227 in **Well Known ID (WKID)** or **European Petroleum Survey Group (EPSG)** systems. More information about these codes is available at `http://spatialreference.org`, a website used to find the thousands of spatial reference systems used throughout the world.

Click on the **Vertical Coordinate Systems** folder and then select the **North America** folder. Select the **North American Vertical Datum of 1988 in feet (NAVD 1988 US survey feet)**. This will make it possible to have the vertical and horizontal linear units in the same measurement system. Click on **Next** to go to the next menu.

The tolerances on the next page are also very important, but we will not cover them in detail here. Accept the defaults and click on **Finish** to finalize the **Feature Dataset**.

Importing the datasets

Import the bus stops, streets, and bus routes feature classes into the `Chapter 11 Results Feature Dataset`. Right-click on the dataset and select **Import**, and then **Feature Class (Single)**. Add the feature classes one by one to give them a new name that will keep them separated from the versions contained within the **SanFrancisco Feature Dataset**. Importing them will make sure that they are in the correct SRS and that a network dataset can be created.

Creating the Network Dataset

Now that we have a data container, we can create a network dataset from the streets feature class. Right-click on the **Chapter11Results** feature dataset and select **New**, and then choose **Network Dataset**.

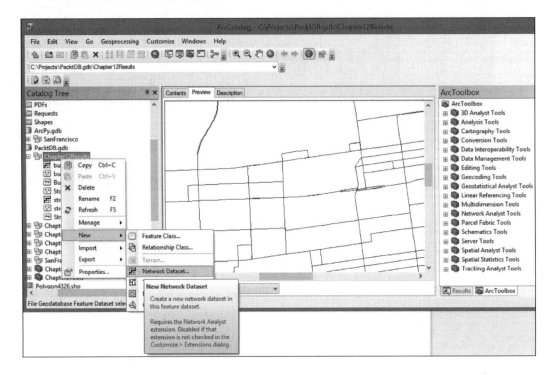

Call the **Network Dataset** Street_Network and click on **Next**. Select the **Streets feature class** as the class that will participate in the network dataset and click on **Next** to move to the next menu. Select **Global Turns** to model turns within the network. In the next menu, use the default connectivity settings. Then, accept the **Using Z Coordinate Values from Geometry** setting. Accept the default cost restriction and driving directions settings, and finally click on **Finish** to generate the network dataset. Then, build the network dataset using the final menu. The network dataset is ready to be used.

Accessing the Network Dataset using ArcPy

Now that the necessary setup has been completed, the street_network network dataset can be added to a script for use in generating routes. Because this is a simple analysis, the only impedance value to be used will be the length of the street segments. Through the use of a `SearchCursor`, `PointGeometry` objects from the bus stops can be accessed and added as locations to be searched:

```
import arcpy
arcpy.CheckOutExtension("Network")
busStops = r'C:\Projects\PacktDB.gdb\Chapter11Results\BusStops'
networkDataset =
r'C:\Projects\PacktDB.gdb\Chapter11Results\street_network'
networkLayer = "streetRoute"
impedance = "Length"
routeFile = "C:\Projects\Layer\{0}.lyr".format(networkLayer)
arcpy.MakeRouteLayer_na(networkDataset,
         networkLayer, impedance)
print 'layer created'
sql = "NAME = '71 IB' AND BUS_SIGNAG = 'Ferry Plaza'"
with arcpy.da.SearchCursor(busStops,['SHAPE@',
                                     'STOPID'],sql) as cursor:
    for row in cursor:
        stopShape = row[0]
        print row[1]
        arcpy.AddLocations_na(networkLayer,'Stops',
            stopShape, "", "")
   arcpy.Solve_na(networkLayer,"SKIP")
arcpy.SaveToLayerFile_management(networkLayer,
             routeLayerFile,"RELATIVE")
print 'finished'
```

Breaking down the script

Let's dissect the script, which once finished, will generate a layer file containing the added Stops, and the Routes along streets to best get from the origin stop to the destination stop.

The script begins by importing the arcPy module. The next line allows us to use the Network Analyst extension:

```
arcpy.CheckOutExtension("Network")
```

Using the `arcpy.CheckOutExtension()` method to invoke the Network Analyst extension involves passing the correct keyword to the method as a parameter. Once it has been invoked, the tools of the extension can be called and executed in the script.

Assigning the bus stops feature class and the street_network network dataset to variables, they can then be passed to ArcPy's `MakeRouteLayer_na()` method, along with a variable representing the impedance value:

```
arcpy.MakeRouteLayer_na(networkDataset,
        networkLayer, impedance)
```

The `MakeRouteLayer_na` tool produces a `RouteLayer` in memory. This blank layer needs to be populated with stops to produce the route(s) between them. For this purpose, we need a `SearchCursor` to access the `PointGeometry` objects and a SQL statement that will limit the returned results to the line of interest:

```
sql = "NAME = '71 IB' AND BUS_SIGNAG = 'Ferry Plaza'"
with arcpy.da.SearchCursor(busStops,['SHAPE@',
                                    'STOPID'],sql) as
cursor:
    for row in cursor:
        stopShape = row[0]
        print row[1]
        arcpy.AddLocations_na(networkLayer,'Stops',stopShape,"", "")
```

The Search Cursor will allow the **Stops** sublayer of the layer produced by the MakeRouteLayer tool to be populated when used in conjunction with the `AddLocations` tool. Once populated, the `RouteLayer` can be passed to the **Solve** tool to find the routes between the points of interest. Again, the routes are solved based on finding the lowest **impedance** between the two points. In this example, the only impedance is the segment length, but it could be traffic or elevation or other restriction types, if that data is available:

```
arcpy.Solve_na(networkLayer,"SKIP")
arcpy.SaveToLayerFile_management(networkLayer,
            routeLayerFile,"RELATIVE")
```

The final result is a layer file that is written to disk using the `SaveToLayerFile` tool.

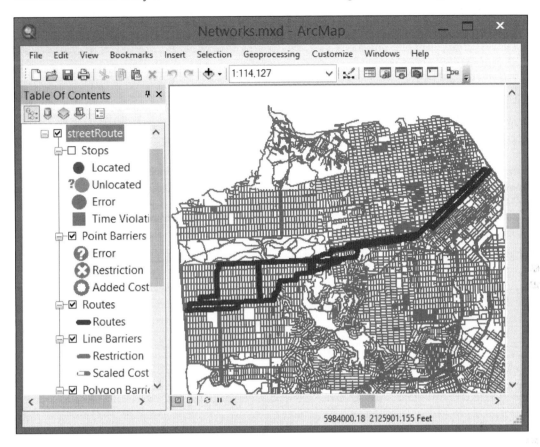

The Network Analyst module

In an effort to make the use of the Network Analyst extension more **Pythonic**, the newer Network Analyst (na) module adjusts how the methods that correspond to the ArcToolbox Network Analyst tools are accessed. Instead of calling the tools directly from ArcPy, the tools are now methods of the na module. Removing the initials of the Network Analyst toolset also reduces confusion and makes it easier to remember the name of the method. See the difference as follows:

```
import arcpy

arcpy.CheckOutExtension("Network")

busStops = r'C:\Projects\SanFrancisco.gdb\SanFrancisco\Bus_Stops'

networkDataset =
r'C:\Projects\SanFrancisco.gdb\Chapter11Results\street_network'
```

```
networkLayer = "streetRoute"

impedance = "Length"

routeLayerFile =
"C:\Projects\Layer\{0}_2.lyr".format(networkLayer) arcpy.na.MakeRouteL
ayer(networkDataset, networkLayer,impedance)

print 'layer created'

sql = "NAME = '71 IB' AND BUS_SIGNAG = 'Ferry Plaza'"

with arcpy.da.SearchCursor(busStops,['SHAPE@',
                'STOPID'],sql) as cursor:

    for row in cursor:

        stopShape = row[0]

        print row[1]

        arcpy.na.AddLocations(networkLayer,'Stops', stopShape, "", "")

arcpy.na.Solve(networkLayer,"SKIP")

arcpy.management.SaveToLayerFile(networkLayer,routeLayerFile,"RELATIVE")

print 'finished'
```

The tool will produce the same layer output as the original script, but the reorganization of the Network Analyst tools into the na module has made the code more logical. For instance, it makes more sense to call Solve using arcpy. na.Solve(), instead of arcpy.Solve_na(), as it reinforces that Solve is a method of the Network Analyst (na) module. As ArcPy continues to be developed, I expect more **Pythonic** code reorganization to occur.

Accessing the Spatial Analyst Extension

The Spatial Analyst Extension is very important to perform analysis on both raster and vector datasets, but it is generally used to perform surface analysis and raster math. These operations are made even easier by the use of ArcPy, as all of the tools available in the Spatial Analyst Toolbox are exposed with the Spatial Analyst access module. This includes the Raster Calculator tools, making map algebra easy by using the tools and operators in simple expressions.

Adding elevation to the bus stops

The elevation raster "sf_elevation" has been downloaded from NOAA and added to the File Geodatabase. However, it covers the entire Bay Area, and we should write a script to only extract an area of the city of San Francisco as it will reduce the time needed to run our scripts. We'll use a SQL statement as the where clause to limit the results to the South of Market (SoMa) neighborhood. To do so, let's take advantage of a Search Cursor and the Spatial Analyst access module's Extract by Polygon property:

```
import arcpy
arcpy.CheckOutExtension("Spatial")
busStops = r'C:\Projects\PacktDB.gdb\SanFrancisco\Bus_Stops'
sanFranciscoHoods = r'C:\Projects\PacktDB.gdb\SanFrancisco\SFFind_
Neighborhoods'
sfElevation = r'C:\Projects\PacktDB.gdb\sf_elevation'
somaGeometry = []
sql = "name = 'South of Market'"
with arcpy.da.SearchCursor(sanFranciscoHoods,['SHAPE@XY'],
        sql,None, True) as cursor:
    for row in cursor:
        X = row[0][0]
        Y = row[0][1]
        somaGeometry.append(arcpy.Point(X,Y))
somaElev = arcpy.sa.ExtractByPolygon(sfElevation,somaGeometry,
"INSIDE")
somaOutPath = sfElevation.replace('sf_elevation','SOMA_elev')
somaElev.save(somaOutPath)
print 'extraction finished'
```

The ExtractByPolygon() method is a bit misleading, as it does not accept a Polygon object as a parameter. Instead, it requires a list of Point objects that represent the vertices of the area that we want to extract. As the SearchCursor is iterating through the neighborhoods dataset, a Polygon object is returned by the cursor. Fortunately, the SearchCursor has a final parameter, which we have not yet explored, that allows us to extract the individual points or vertices that make up the Soma neighborhood polygon. By setting the Search Cursor's optional Explode to Points parameter (which converts Polygon objects into coordinate pairs for each vertex) to True, Point objects can be generated by passing the XY values of each returned vertex to the arcpy.Point method. These Point() objects are appended to the somaGeometry list and then passed to the Spatial Analyst access module's ExtractByPolygon method.

Passing a Polygon Object instead of Point Objects will return an error.

Using Map Algebra to generate elevation in feet

We now have a raster to use to extract elevation values. However, both the original raster and the generated SoMa neighborhood raster contain elevation values in meters, and it would be better to convert them to feet to keep them consistent with the projection of the bus stops. Let's use raster math and the `Times()` method to convert the values from meters to feet:

```
somaOutPath = sfElevation.replace('sf_elevation','SOMA_elev')

outTimes = arcpy.sa.Times(somaOutPath, 3.28084)

somaFeetOutPath = sfElevation.replace('sf_elevation','SOMA_feet')

outTimes.save(somaFeetOutPath)
```

The `Times()` method generates a new raster to glean the elevation values we need for the bus stops of interest.

Adding in the bus stops and getting elevation values

Now that we have generated a raster that we can use to find elevation values in feet, we need to add a new `arcpy.sa()` method to generate the points. The `ExtractValuesToPoints()` method will generate a new bus stops feature class with a new field that holds the elevation values:

```
with arcpy.da.SearchCursor(sanFranciscoHoods,['SHAPE@'],sql) as cursor:
    for row in cursor:
        somaPoly = row[0]
arcpy.MakeFeatureLayer_management(busStops, 'soma_stops')
arcpy.SelectLayerByLocation_management("soma_stops",
                                "INTERSECT",somaPoly)
outStops = r'C:\Projects\PacktDB.gdb\Chapter11Results\SoMaStops'
arcpy.sa.ExtractValuesToPoints("soma_stops", somaOutFeet,
                                outStops,"INTERPOLATE",
                                "VALUE_ONLY")

print 'points generated'
```

The final result

We produced a subset feature class of the bus stops that has the elevation values added as a field. This process could be repeated for the entire city, one neighborhood at a time, or it could be performed with the original elevation raster on the entire bus stops feature class to generate a value for each stop:

```
import arcpy
arcpy.CheckOutExtension("Spatial")
arcpy.env.overwriteOutput = True
busStops = r'C:\Projects\PacktDB.gdb\SanFrancisco\Bus_Stops'
sanFranciscoHoods = r'C:\Projects\SanFrancisco.gdb\SanFrancisco\SFFind_
Neighborhoods'
sfElevation = r'C:\Projects\SanFrancisco.gdb\sf_elevation'


somaGeometry = []
sql = "name = 'South of Market'"
with arcpy.da.SearchCursor(sanFranciscoHoods,['SHAPE@XY'],
            sql,None, True) as cursor:
    for row in cursor:
        somaGeometry.append(arcpy.Point(row[0][0],row[0][1]))
somaElev = arcpy.sa.ExtractByPolygon(sfElevation, somaGeometry,
                                "INSIDE")
somaOutput = sfElevation.replace('sf_elevation','SOMA_elev')
somaElev.save(somaOutput)
print 'extraction finished'


somaOutput = sfElevation.replace('sf_elevation','SOMA_elev')
outTimes = arcpy.sa.Times(somaOutput, 3.28084)
somaOutFeet = sfElevation.replace('sf_elevation','SOMA_feet')
outTimes.save(somaOutFeet)
print 'conversion complete'


with arcpy.da.SearchCursor(sanFranciscoHoods,['SHAPE@'],sql) as cursor:
    for row in cursor:
        somaPoly = row[0]


arcpy.MakeFeatureLayer_management(busStops, 'soma_stops')
```

```
arcpy.SelectLayerByLocation_management("soma_stops", "INTERSECT",
                                       somaPoly)


outStops = r'C:\Projects\SanFrancisco.gdb\Chapter11Results\SoMaStops'
arcpy.sa.ExtractValuesToPoints("soma_stops", somaOutFeet,
                               outStops,"INTERPOLATE",
                               "VALUE_ONLY")
print 'points generated'
```

This script demonstrates well the value of accessing the advanced extensions in ArcPy and combining them with SearchCursors and Geometry objects. The script could be taken even further by adding a SearchCursor to look through the outstops dataset and exporting the results to a spreadsheet, or even adding a new field to the original bus stops dataset to populate with the elevation values. It could even be used as impedance values to be entered into a Network Analyst extension analysis — a fun coding task that I hope you will attempt.

Summary

In this chapter, we covered the basics of using common ArcGIS for Desktop Advanced extensions within ArcPy, with a focus on the Network Analyst access module and the Spatial Analyst access module. We explored how to generate a network and how to create network paths using ArcPy. We also explored how to access Spatial Analyst tools and use them in conjunction with SearchCursors to work with rasters and vectors for spatial analysis.

In the next chapter, we will explore some final pieces to the ArcPy puzzle that will allow the creation of advanced scripts and script tools.

12
The End of the Beginning

This book is almost done, but there is so much more to know about writing code in Python and ArcPy. Unfortunately, I can't fit it all into one book, but that also means that you get to have fun exploring all of the methods and properties of ArcPy. As a conclusion to the book, we will cover some other important topics that can crop up when writing ArcPy scripts. Combined with the lessons from earlier chapters, I hope you'll soon be using ArcPy at work, at school, or just for fun (why not?).

This chapter will cover the following topics:

- Working with field information – types, aliases, domains, spatial types, and more
- Accessing information describing a Feature Class
- Automatically generating a Feature Class and populating it with fields
- Automatically creating File Geodatabases and Feature Datasets
- Creating a Script tool that will run the bus stop analysis and generate results in an automatically generated File Geodatabase, Feature Dataset, and Feature Class

Getting field information from feature classes

When creating script tools, or just running a script, there can be times that extracting field information from a feature class (or shapefile) is necessary. This information can include field names and aliases, field type and length, scale, domains, or subtypes. These are all properties available through the `arcpy.ListFields` method. We'll explore the many properties, how to extract them, and how to use them in a script.

By organizing the ArcPy methods into a function, the data is organized in a form that we prefer, instead of relying on the default organization used by the designers of ArcPy. It's important to remember that scripts you create should reflect your needs, and creating these function **wrappers** is one step forward towards polishing the raw ArcPy tools to work in your workflows.

Accessing the ListFields' properties

The List Fields tool is available as an ArcPy method. `Arcpy.ListFields` accepts only one parameter, a feature class, or shapefile. Once the parameter has been passed, a series of important properties are available using dot notation. To take further advantage of these properties, we will create functions that make it easy to get the information we want, in the format we require.

List comprehensions

Within these field information functions, we will take advantage of a Python data structure known as list comprehensions. They simplify the `for` loop structure to make it easier to populate a list with the values required (the field information in this case).

To create a list comprehension, a `for` loop is generated inside a set of brackets, and the list is populated with the generated values. Here is an example of a list comprehension that creates a list with the square values of the numbers from 1 to 10, as run in the Python interpreter:

```
>>>originalList = range(1,11)
>>>print originalList
[1, 2, 3, 4, 5, 6, 7, 8, 9, 10]
>>>newList =  [x**2 for x in originalList]
>>>print newList
[1, 4, 9, 16, 25, 36, 49, 64, 81, 100]
```

List comprehensions are used because they are faster and easier to write, though it may take some time to get used to the syntax. Experiment with them to better understand their use and limitations, and also consult some of the many resources available online.

Creating the field information functions

Each of the functions will be a separate entity, but they will all have a similar structure. One parameter will be accepted by each function, the feature class of interest. ArcPy will be imported, and later deleted from memory, to make sure that the `ListFields()` method can be called without an error. Once the feature class is passed to the `ListFields()` method, the values desired will populate a list inside a list comprehension. Once it has been populated, it is returned from the function using the return keyword.

Here is the set of functions for the field names:

```
def returnfieldnames(fc):
    import arcpy
    fieldnames = [f.name for f in arcpy.ListFields(fc)]
    del arcpy
    return fieldnames


def returnfieldalias(fc):
    import arcpy
    fieldalias = [f.aliasName for f in arcpy.ListFields(fc)]
    del arcpy
    return fieldalias


def returnfieldbasename(fc):
    import arcpy
    fieldtypes = [f.baseName for f in arcpy.ListFields(fc)]
    del arcpy
    return fieldtypes
```

These name functions are useful when creating a new feature class based on another feature class. Sometimes there is a need to preserve the exact names and aliases from the original feature class, and using these functions will make this possible. When doing this, there is a need to provide other field information as well. Here are the functions related to field types, lengths, precision, and scale:

```
def returnfieldtypes(fc):
    import arcpy
    fieldtypes = [f.type for f in arcpy.ListFields(fc)]
    del arcpy
```

```
        return fieldtypes


def returnfieldlength(fc):
    import arcpy
    fieldlengths = [f.length for f in arcpy.ListFields(fc)]
    del arcpy
    return fieldlengths


def returnfieldprecision(fc):
    import arcpy
    fieldprecise = [f.precision for f in arcpy.ListFields(fc)]
    del arcpy
    return fieldprecise


def returnfieldscale(fc):
    import arcpy
    fieldscales = [f.scale for f in arcpy.ListFields(fc)]
    del arcpy
    return fieldscales
```

There is even a property used to request domain information:

```
def returnfielddomain(fc):
    import arcpy
    fielddomains = [f.domain for f in arcpy.ListFields(fc)]
    del arcpy
    return fielddomains
```

These functions all share the structure discussed earlier, and have the advantage of being simple to use and easy to search throughout. Because fields in a feature class have a specific order, each list returned by the functions will have an order to the information returned, accessible by a specific index number.

The fieldsubtypes are also available through the data access module. Because they are related to the fields, they are returned as a dictionary:

```
def returnfieldsubtypes(fc):
    import arcpy
    fieldsubdic = {}
    subtypes = arcpy.da.ListSubtypes(fc)
```

```
for stcode, stdict in subtypes.iteritems():
    for stkey in stdict.iterkeys():
        if stkey == 'FieldValues':
            fields = stdict[stkey]
            for field, fieldvals in fields.iteritems():
                sub = fieldvals[0]
                desc = fieldvals[1]
                fieldsubdic[field] = sub, desc


del arcpy
return fieldsubdic
```

Adding these functions to the useful.py script in the common module will make them available to any script or script tool. Use the import keyword to add them to any new script. They are self-contained functions that only require the file path to the feature class of interest.

Querying feature class information

Some important pieces of information about an incoming feature class cannot be accessed using the ListFields() method. Instead, a number of different methods will be used to find the Geometry type, or Spatial Reference, or the field subtype of each feature class. Some of these are discovered using ArcPy's Describe method, built to provide

For the Geometry type, we will use the shapeType property of the Describe() method:

```
def returngeometrytype(fc):
    import arcpy
    arcInfo = arcpy.Describe(fc)
    geomtype = arcInfo.shapeType
    del arcpy
    return str(geomtype)
```

The name of the Shape field (which usually defaults to Shape) can also be requested using the Describe method and returns a string data type:

```
def returngeometryname(fc):
    import arcpy
```

```
arcInfo = arcpy.Describe(fc)

geomname = arcInfo.shapeFieldName

del arcpy

return str(geomname)
```

The feature class `spatial_reference` is also available through the `Describe` method. The data is returned as a `spatial_reference` object:

```
def returnspatialreference(fc):

    import arcpy

    spatial_reference = arcpy.Describe(fc).spatialReference

    del arcpy

    return spatial_reference
```

A `spatial_reference` object has a number of important properties. The `projectionname` and `projectioncode` are among the important

```
def returnprojectioncode(fc):

    import arcpy

    spatial_reference = arcpy.Describe(fc).spatialReference

    proj_code = spatial_reference.projectionCode

    del arcpy

    return  proj_code
```

```
def returnprojectionname(fc):

    import arcpy

    spatial_reference = arcpy.Describe(fc).spatialReference

    proj_name = spatial_reference.name

    del arcpy

    return  proj_name
```

Many other properties and methods can be similarly utilized to make them available within scripts or script tools. Explore the ArcGIS help documents for further insights into the properties available through the `Describe` method.

Generating File Geodatabases and feature classes

File Geodatabases do not have to exist before a script is run; instead, they can be generated when a script is executed using the `CreateFileGDB` tool, which is also an ArcPy method. Once the `File` Geodatabase has been created, `Feature Datasets` can be added.

Generating the File Geodatabase is very easy. The only parameters are the folders to place it inside, and the name of the Geodatabase:

```
import arcpy
folderPath = r"C:\Projects"
gdbName = "ArcPy.gdb"
arcpy.CreateFileGDB_management(folderPath, gdbName)
```

The Feature Datasets are more difficult to create, as there is an optional spatial reference parameter that requires a Spatial Reference object to be generated. While the Spatial Reference object is optional, it is highly recommended.

There are a few options to generate the `SpatialReference` object. One of them uses the `return specialReference()` function defined earlier; by passing a feature class to the function, a Spatial Reference object is created. Another method would be to pass a file path to a projection file `.prj` as the optional third parameter. A third method is to generate a Spatial Reference object by using the `arcpy.SpatialReference` method and passing it a projection code or a projection string:

```
spatialReference = arcpy.SpatialReference(2227)
```

However it is generated, it is then passed to the `arcpy.CreateFeatureDataset` method along with the file path of the File Geodatabase and the name of the Feature Dataset:

```
spatialReference = arcpy.SpatialReference(2227)
fileGDB = r"{0}\{1}".format(folderPath,gdbName)
featureDataset = "Chapter12Results"
arcpy.CreateFeatureDataset_management(fileGDB, featureDataset,
                                      spatialReference)
```

Generating a feature class

Now that a File Geodatabase and a Feature Dataset have been created, let's generate a Feature Class inside the Feature Dataset. This is done using the `arcpy.` `CreateFeatureClass` method. This method has a number of optional parameters, including a Feature Class to use as a template and a Spatial Reference. For this example, there is no need to use the Spatial Reference parameter as it is being written to a Feature Dataset, which dictates the Spatial Reference used. The template parameter will copy the fields of the template Feature Class, but for now, we will only create the Shape field:

```
featureClass = "BufferArea"

geometryType = "POLYGON"

featurePath = r"{0}\{1}".format(fileGDB,featureDataset)

arcpy.CreateFeatureclass_management(featurePath, featureClass,
                                    geometryType)
```

The created Feature Class will need some fields with the attribute information that will be populated later. The fields have a number of parameters that depend on the field type, including length, precision, and alias, among others:

```
fieldName = "STOPID"

fieldAlias = "Bus Stop Identifier"

fieldType = "LONG"

fieldPrecision = 9

featureClassPath = r"{0}\{1}".format(featurePath,featureClass)

arcpy.AddField_management(featureClassPath, fieldName,
                          fieldType, fieldPrecision,"", "", fieldAlias)
```

Let's add a second field to hold the averaged population values produced by the Bus Stop analysis:

```
fieldName2 = "AVEPOP"

fieldAlias2 = "Average Census Population"

fieldType2 = "FLOAT"

featureClassPath = r"{0}\{1}".format(featurePath,featureClass)

arcpy.AddField_management(featureClassPath, fieldName2, fieldType2, "",
                          "", "", fieldAlias2)
```

The File Geodatabase, Feature Dataset, and Feature Class fields have now been generated. Let's extend the script into a script tool by adding the Bus Stop analysis functions, while writing the results to the generated **Feature Class**. Creating, a script tool that populates a feature class.

This script tool will borrow from the ideas outlined in *Chapter 10*, *Advanced Geometry Object Methods* and will create a union of the Polygon Geometry objects that intersect with the buffered bus stops to populate the **Shape field**, along with the **bus stop ID** and the averaged population for the blocks intersected with each buffer.

Open the script `Chapter12_3.py` and explore its contents. Coupled with the code snippets mentioned earlier and the use of `arcpy.GetParameterAsText` to get data from the script tool, the data generated will be written in a feature class by the following code:

```python
arcpy.AddMessage("Beginning Analysis")

insertCursor = arcpy.da.InsertCursor(featureClassPath,
                            ['SHAPE@',fieldName, fieldName2])

arcpy.MakeFeatureLayer_management(censusBlocks2010,"census_lyr")


with arcpy.da.SearchCursor(busStops, ['SHAPE@', busStopField],sql) as
cursor:
    for row in cursor:
        stop = row[0]
        stopID = row[1]
        busBuffer = stop.buffer(400)
        arcpy.SelectLayerByLocation_management("census_lyr","intersect",
                                        busBuffer,'',
                                        'NEW_SELECTION')
        censusShapes = []
        censusPopList = []
        with arcpy.da.SearchCursor("census_lyr", ['SHAPE@',
                            censusBlockPopField]) as ncursor:
            for nrow in ncursor:
                censusShapes.append(nrow[0])
                censusPopList.append(nrow[1])


        censusUnion = censusShapes[0]
        for block in censusShapes[1:]:
```

```
        censusUnion = censusUnion.union(block)


    censusPop = sum(censusPopList)/len(censusPopList)

    finalData = (censusUnion,stopID, censusPopulation)

    insertCursor.insertRow(finalData)

arcpy.AddMessage("Analysis Complete")
```

The script combines many of the ideas that have been introduced throughout the book to allow the user to run a complete workflow that generates a feature class containing the results of the analysis. By adding only the fields of interest and populating them with the unioned `Polygon` objects, the script eliminates most of the cruft, normally created when running a spatial analysis, and produces a results dataset that can be viewed in ArcMap.

Setting up the script tool parameters

Here is how the parameters of the script tool look when set up:

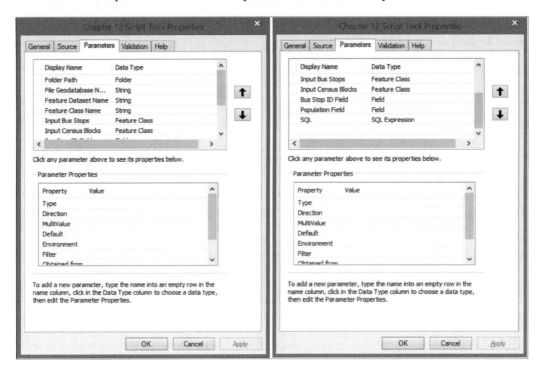

The list of parameters is long, so I am using two images to portray them. It is important to choose the correct data type for each parameter as it will control the dialog generated to retrieve the data.

The **bus stop ID field** and the **Population** field are both obtained from their respective feature classes. The **File Geodatabase** name is a string and the code will append .gdb to the end of the input string if it is not entered initially, to make sure that it can be correctly generated. It should not already exist; it will not be generated if it does (if desired, this can be changed by setting the arcpy.env. overwriteOutput property to True after the import statement).

Once the parameters have been set, and the tool has a name and description, save it and then open the tool. It should look like this once it has been filled out:

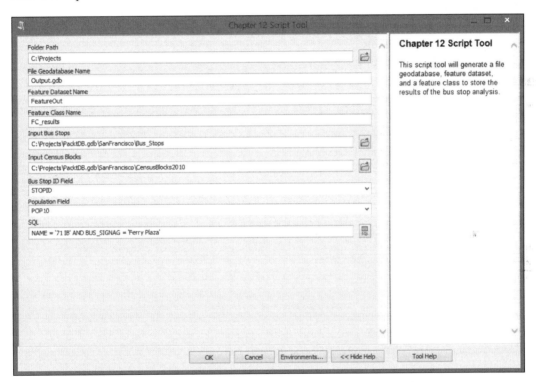

Click on **OK** to run the tool. Open **ArcMap** and add the results, along with the San Francisco polygon and the Inbound71 feature class from *Chapter 4, Complex ArcPy Scripts and Generalizing Functions*. The results will look similar to this, after a bit of cartographic symbolizing:

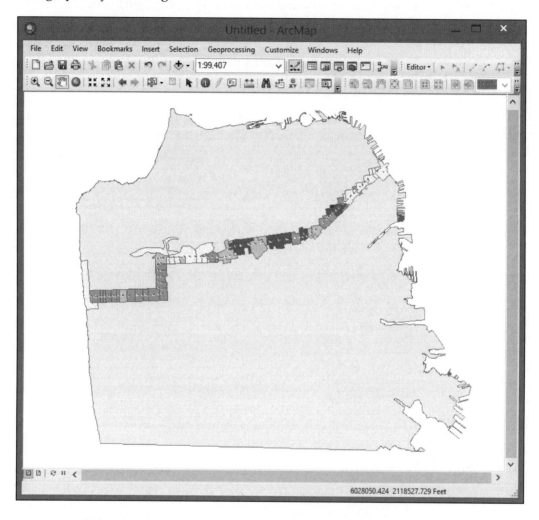

The final result will have one row per bus stop selected, along with the averaged population and the bus stop ID value. Instead of using a spreadsheet as an output, the feature class will allow to make maps or produce further spatial analysis. Producing custom data using custom script tools puts you in the driver's seat when performing geospatial analyses and makes your tools, and you, a valuable asset to any team.

Environmental settings

The ArcPy module allows for the control of global settings that controls input and output processes using ArcPy's env class. These settings will have an effect on the accuracy of data produced using geospatial analysis tools. Resolution and tolerance settings for *X*, *Y*, *Z*, and *M* coordinates can be controlled, along with output extent, raster cell size, analysis workspace, and many other settings.

To access the environmental settings using ArcPy, the class env is imported from arcpy:

```
>>> from arcpy import env
```

It can also be called using dot notation shown as follows. Setting the workspace removes the need to pass a file path to any subsequent methods called on the workspace. Here is an example of setting the workspace and calling the ListDatasets() method without passing a file path as a parameter:

```
>>> import arcpy
>>> arcpy.env.workspace = r"C:\Projects\SanFrancisco.gdb"
>>> arcpy.ListDatasets()

[u'SanFrancisco', u'Chapter3Results', u'Chapter4Results',
u'Chapter5Results', u'Chapter7Results', u'Chapter11Results']
```

Resolution and tolerance settings

The resolution and tolerance settings control the accuracy of the output of any data produced by a tool in ArcToolbox or when running a script using ArcPy. These can (and should) be set for Feature Datasets in File Geodatabases or Enterprise Geodatabases, but it is important to set them for analysis run in the memory or when using shapefiles, or if the geospatial analysis requires greater accuracy than used by those Geodatabases.

Setting the resolutions and tolerances require an understanding of the accuracy required for your projects. These settings will limit the ability to snap to a line or find points that intersect with a line. The linear unit will need to reflect the coordinate system of choice:

```
import arcpy
arcpy.env.MResolution = 0.0005
arcpy.env.MTolerance = 0.005
arcpy.env.ZResolution = "0.0025 Feet"
```

```
arcpy.env.ZTolerance = "0.001 Feet"

arcpy.env.XYResolution = "0.00025 Feet"

arcpy.env.XYTolerance = "0.0005 Feet"
```

Other important environmental settings include:

- The **Extent** setting, which limits the extent of any data produced from an analysis by setting a rectangle of interest using an `Extent` object, or a string with space delimited coordinates (`Xmin`, `Ymin`, `Xmax`, `Ymax`) in the current coordinate system.

- The **Mask** setting, which limits raster analysis to areas that intersect with a feature class or a raster passed as a string file path parameter to the setting.

- The **Cell Size** setting, which controls the cell size of the data produced using raster analysis.

Take time and explore the powerful ArcPy Environmental Settings to reduce the time needed to write code and ensure high-quality data production.

Summary

This chapter and this book have demonstrated some of the many ways that ArcPy can be used to automate geospatial analysis. By applying the lessons, and by being creative with the many methods and properties of ArcPy, repetitive and slow geospatial processes can be scripted and made into custom tools that will save a lot of time.

I hope that you enjoyed learning the basics of scripting with ArcPy and Python. I really hope that you've even come to like the idea of programming, as it is powerful and empowering. There is much more to master, but I think you will find that the more scripting you do, the easier it is to understand.

The best resource for further understanding of ArcPy is the ArcGIS Help Documents, available through the Help menu in ArcCatalog or ArcMap. The documentation is also available at `http://resources.arcgis.com/en/help/main/10.2/index.html`. Working on entering the correct question into Google can be very helpful as well. Programming forums such as Stack Exchange (`http://gis.stackexchange.com/`) or ESRI's GeoNet (`https://geonet.esri.com/welcome`) are valuable resources to ask all kinds of programming questions. There is an answer for almost every question you may have (but never be afraid to ask questions yourself!).

Have fun creating solutions and tools, and good luck in all your future geospatial programming challenges!

Index

C

census block
and bus stop buffer block, intersecting 141
Census Block feature class
adding, as parameter 118
Census Block field
adding, as parameter 118
Comma Separated Value (CSV) 119
CSV module
adding, to script 54, 55
cursor
used, for accessing data 55-57

D

data
accessing, cursor used 55-57
data access module
about 82-85
attribute field interactions 85
insert cursor, using 89, 90
point location, adjusting 87, 88
row, deleting with update cursor 88
shape field, updating 87
update cursor 86
data frame window extent
controlling 152
datasets
importing 177
data sources
replacing 140
data types
about 15
adding 116
dictionaries 18, 19
floats 17
integers 16
iterable data types 19, 20
lists 17
strings 16
tuples 18
definition query 149-151
def keyword 21
deleteRow method 88
dictionaries 18, 19

dynamic components
adding, to script 111, 112
dynamic parameters
adding, to script 109, 110

E

environmental settings
about 199
Cell Size setting 200
Extent setting 200
Mask setting 200
resolution setting 199, 200
tolerance setting 199, 200

F

feature classes
environmental settings 199
feature class information, querying 191, 192
field information functions,
creating 189, 190
field information, obtaining from 187, 188
File Geodatabases, generating 193
generating 193-195
List comprehensions 188
List Fields tool 188
script tool parameters, setting up 196-198
feature class information
querying 191, 192
Feature Dataset
creating 176, 177
field information
obtaining, from feature classes 187, 188
field information functions
creating 189, 190
file paths, in Python 48
final script
about 57
inspecting 123-126
floats 17
for loops 13
functions
about 21
used, within script 164-170

G

geometry objects 103, 104
GIS 15

H

hard-coded inputs 109

I

IDEs
  about 30, 35
  Aptana Studio 3 33-35
  automatically generated script 46, 47
  IDLE 30, 31
  PythonWin 31, 32
IDLE 30, 31
individual layers
  fixing 130, 131
insert cursor
  using 89, 90
integers 16
Integrated Development
          Environments. *See* IDEs
Intersect tool
  adding 44
iterable data types 19, 20

K

keyword method 88
keywords 21

L

Layer object
  adding 153, 154
  controlling, arcpy.mapping used 147, 148
  methods 148
  properties 148
layer sources
  broken links, fixing 129
  individual layers, fixing 130, 131
  inspecting 128

map document elements,
          adjusting 131-134
  replacing 128
layer visibility
  adjusting 140

M

map documents
  ArcPy, using with 128
  elements, adjusting 131-134
maps
  creating 127
  exporting 154
model
  analysis results, tallying 45
  Buffer tool, modeling 43
  creating 42
  exporting 46
  exporting, to Python 42
  Intersect tool, adding 44
  Select tool, modeling 43
module
  adding, sys module used 37
  residing 37

N

namespaces 21
naming variables
  using, best practices 12
Network Analyst
  datasets, importing 177
  extension 175
  Feature Dataset, creating 176, 177
  module 181, 182
  network dataset access, ArcPy used 179
  network dataset, creating 178
  using 176
network dataset
  creating 178

O

Operating System (OS) module 23
output spreadsheet
  adding, as parameter 119

P

parameter
Bus Stop feature class, adding as 117
bus stop fields, adding as 122
Census Block feature class, adding as 118
Census Block field, adding as 118
data types, adding 116
output spreadsheet, adding as 119
spreadsheet field names, adding as 120
SQL Statement, adding as 121
PDF
adjusted map, exporting to 143
PointGeometry objects 104-107
point location
adjusting 87
polygon geometry
inserting 91, 92
Polygon object methods 161, 162
Polygon objects 100-103
polyline geometry
inserting 90, 91
Python, as programming language
about 8
glue language 9
interpreted language 8
standard (built-in) library 9
wrapper modules 9
Python, basics
about 10
comments 15
for loops 13
import statements 11
variables 12
while statement 14
Python folder structure
about 36
modules, residing 37
sys module used, for adding module 37
Python functions
about 61
defining 62
generalization 74-77
used, for replacing repetitive code 65-73
with parameters 63, 64
writing 63

Python interpreter
about 26
locating 28, 29
location 27
using 27
Python module
__init__.py file 158-161
creating 157, 158
Python script
about 25
executing 26
PythonWin
about 31, 32
URL 31
Python window
script, running in 144

R

random points
generating, to represent population 163
replace() method 86
row
deleting, with update cursor 88

S

scale properties
controlling 152
script
adjusting 46, 54
breaking 179, 180
CSV module, adding to 54, 55
dynamic components, adding to 111, 112
dynamic parameters, adding to 109, 110
running, in Python Window 144
script analysis, ArcPy Tools
continuing 49
Intersect Tool 50
string manipulation 50
script messages
displaying, arcpy.AddMessage used 110
script tool
creating 112-115
parameters, defining 115
parameters, labeling 115

script tool parameters
  setting up 196-198
Select tool
  modeling 43
shape field
  updating 87
Spatial Analyst Extension
  accessing 182
  bus stops, adding 184-186
  elevation, adding to bus stops 183
  elevation values, obtaining 184-186
  Map Algebra used, for generating elevation
    in feet 184
spreadsheet field names
  adding, as parameter 120
SQL Statement
  adding, as parameter 121
standard library modules
  csv 24
  datetime 24
  math 24
  string 24
string addition 51
string formatting 52, 53
string manipulation
  string addition 51
  string formatting 52, 53
strings 16
subroutines 62
sys module
  used, for adding module 37

T

text elements
  adjusted map, exporting to PDF 143
  updating 143
Tkinter 31
tuples 18

U

update cursor
  about 86, 87
  used, for deleting row 88
updateRow() method 87

W

while statement 14

X

XLRD module 23
XLS
  creating, XLWT used 170-172
XLWT module 23

Z

zero-based indexing 22

Thank you for buying
ArcPy and ArcGIS – Geospatial Analysis with Python

About Packt Publishing

Packt, pronounced 'packed', published its first book, *Mastering phpMyAdmin for Effective MySQL Management*, in April 2004, and subsequently continued to specialize in publishing highly focused books on specific technologies and solutions.

Our books and publications share the experiences of your fellow IT professionals in adapting and customizing today's systems, applications, and frameworks. Our solution-based books give you the knowledge and power to customize the software and technologies you're using to get the job done. Packt books are more specific and less general than the IT books you have seen in the past. Our unique business model allows us to bring you more focused information, giving you more of what you need to know, and less of what you don't.

Packt is a modern yet unique publishing company that focuses on producing quality, cutting-edge books for communities of developers, administrators, and newbies alike. For more information, please visit our website at www.packtpub.com.

About Packt Open Source

In 2010, Packt launched two new brands, Packt Open Source and Packt Enterprise, in order to continue its focus on specialization. This book is part of the Packt Open Source brand, home to books published on software built around open source licenses, and offering information to anybody from advanced developers to budding web designers. The Open Source brand also runs Packt's Open Source Royalty Scheme, by which Packt gives a royalty to each open source project about whose software a book is sold.

Writing for Packt

We welcome all inquiries from people who are interested in authoring. Book proposals should be sent to author@packtpub.com. If your book idea is still at an early stage and you would like to discuss it first before writing a formal book proposal, then please contact us; one of our commissioning editors will get in touch with you.

We're not just looking for published authors; if you have strong technical skills but no writing experience, our experienced editors can help you develop a writing career, or simply get some additional reward for your expertise.

Building Web and Mobile ArcGIS Server Applications with JavaScript

ISBN: 978-1-84969-796-5   Paperback: 274 pages

Master the ArcGIS API for JavaScript, and build exciting, custom web and mobile GIS applications with the ArcGIS Server

1. Develop ArcGIS Server applications with JavaScript, both for traditional web browsers as well as the mobile platform.

2. Acquire in-demand GIS skills sought by many employers.

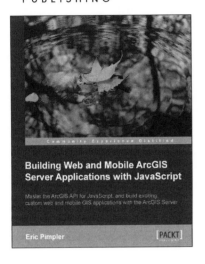

Administering ArcGIS for Server

ISBN: 978-1-78217-736-4   Paperback: 246 pages

Installing and configuring ArcGIS for Server to publish, optimize, and secure GIS services

1. Configure ArcGIS for Server to achieve maximum performance and response time.

2. Understand the product mechanics to build up good troubleshooting skills.

3. Filled with practical exercises, examples, and code snippets to help facilitate your learning.

Please check **www.PacktPub.com** for information on our titles

14769522R00125

Printed in Great Britain
by Amazon.co.uk, Ltd.,
Marston Gate.